KV-277-000

EVERYDAY LIFE OF ANIMALS

THE SEARCH FOR FOOD

Text by Marco Ferrari

Illustrations by Ivan Stalio

CHERRYTREE BOOKS

In the same series:

Adapting to the Environment

Life Cycles

The Animal Atlas

THE SEARCH FOR FOOD

Text by Marco Ferrari
Consultant Fulvio Cerfolli
Illustrations by Ivan Stalio, Antonella Pastorelli,
Marco Sparaciari
Translated by Elizabeth Foody, Anne McRae,
Darryl Price
Graphic design by Marco Nardi

Copyright © 1998 McRae Books, Florence

English edition published by Cherrytree Press Ltd,
Windsor Bridge Road, Bath BA2 3AX

Copyright © Cherrytree Press Ltd 1998

British Library Cataloguing in Publication Data.

Ferrari, Marco
    The search for food. – (Everyday life of animals)
    1. Animals – Food – Juvenile literature
    I. Title
    591.5'3

    ISBN 0 7451 5293 7

Colour separations by R.A.F. (Florence)

Printed in Italy by Grafiche Editoriali Padane, Cremona

All rights reserved. No part of this publication may be
reproduced, stored in a retrieval system or transmitted,
in any form or by any means, without prior permission
in writing of the copyright holder, nor be otherwise
circulated in any form of binding or cover other than
that in which it is published and without a similar
condition including this condition being imposed on
the subsequent purchaser.

CONTENTS

INTRODUCTION

A cheetah in hot pursuit of a gazelle, a wolf pack closing in on a deer, a spider lying in wait for a fly, and a monkey cramming berries into its mouth are all players in a drama that takes place every day in the animal world – the unending search for food. All animals have to eat in order to get energy for living. They eat plants or other animals, and each kind of animal has its favourite food and its own special way of getting it. Over millions of years, the processes of evolution have created a huge variety of fascinating methods of catching food. Some meateaters or carnivores undertake long-distance chases, while others grab their prey with lightning-fast strikes: some lie in wait for unwary victims, and some fishes use bait to attract them. A few carnivores, including many spiders, even make traps to snare their prey. Wolves hunt in packs, with each member having a particular task and knowing just what to do. Almost all living creatures can be another animal's dinner, but animals don't just sit around waiting to be eaten. Most of them have some kind of defence: some escape simply because they are faster than their enemies, some protect themselves with spines, horns or other weapons, and others employ camouflage – colours and patterns that blend in with the surroundings and make the animals difficult to see. Some are actually poisonous. The predators have to be fast or very clever to catch their food. Even plants can protect themselves: many have spines or poisonous juices that deter herbivores (plant-eating animals). But even the best defences cannot protect against all enemies. Many animals have tough jaws that break down the defences, or special digestive juices that destroy the poisons.

An animal's metabolism determines how much food it needs. Reptiles and amphibians are fairly slow-moving, cold-blooded creatures and they can make do with much less food than birds and mammals of the same size – because birds and mammals are very active, warm-blooded creatures and need a lot of energy.

The Search for Food takes a look at the wide variety of methods that animals use to find and capture their food, and also at the many ways by which they avoid being eaten themselves. It presents a fascinating picture of the complex food chains and webs that link animals and plants together and keep nature in balance all over the world.

The giraffe's long neck and tongue are special adaptations for reaching the topmost leaves on the acacia tree.

SURVIVAL OF THE FITTEST

During the millions of years that animals have been on the earth, they have had to compete with each other for food. Many species lost the struggle and died out. Only the fittest or most efficient kinds of animals have survived. Each one has become adapted to a particular sort of food, so the earth's food resources are efficiently shared out and all the animals normally get enough to eat. Most animals are either planteaters (herbivores) or meateaters (carnivores). In any ecosystem (a community of plants and animals living in a particular area), nature ensures that there are enough planteaters to feed the meateaters, but not so many that they eat all the plants. If the planteaters get too common they will destroy the plants, and then starve unless they can move off to find food somewhere else. The meateaters then have to move or starve as well. Each kind of animal has evolved efficient senses for finding its food. It also has effective equipment for catching or collecting it and the right processes for digesting the food and making the best use of it. The teeth of meat-eating mammals, for example, are very different from the teeth of planteaters. As well as having to find food, animals have to avoid being eaten, so they try to stay one jump ahead of their enemies. For example, if a big cat evolves into a faster creature it will be able to catch more prey. But nature will then encourage the evolution of even faster prey to restore the balance. If this did not happen, the prey would die out – and the predator would then have nothing to eat.

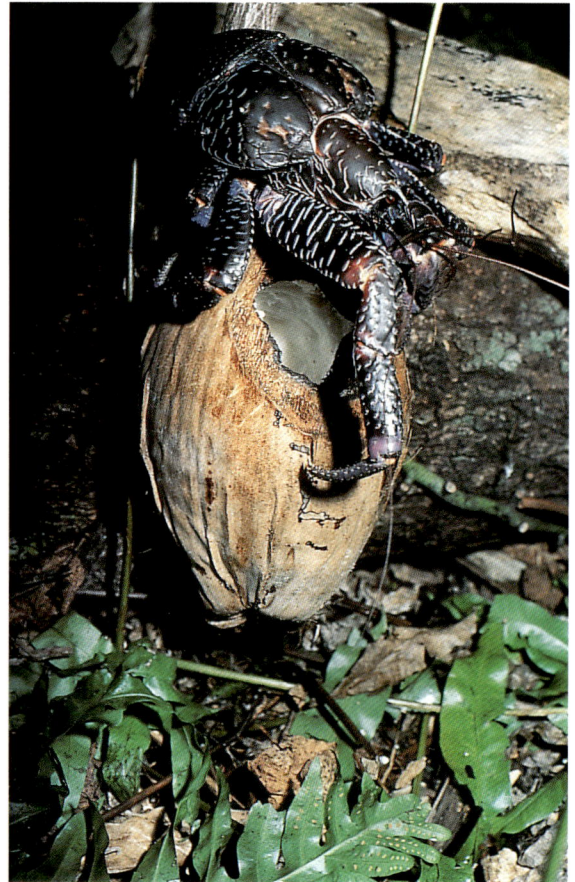

FINDING FOOD IN PALM TREES
The coconut crab, or robber crab, lives on tropical beaches. Unlike most other crabs, it spends most of its time on land. It lives in burrows and holes in trees, sometimes quite far from the sea. It uses its big, strong claws to tear up the flesh of dead animals. It also digs out the flesh of broken coconuts on the beach. Coconut crabs are well adapted to life on land; their gills have been replaced by lungs and if they stay in the water too long they will drown. Like other land animals, the crabs drink fresh water from inland springs and streams. They also climb trees to feed on juicy berries.

Horse

Egg-eating snake

Horned frog

Shark

Puma

Mussel

Hare

THE RIGHT MOUTH FOR THE RIGHT FOOD

The size and shape of an animal's mouth are closely linked to its food. Animals that swallow their food whole need large mouths that will open very wide, like the egg-eating snake or the horned frog. Sharp, strong teeth for grasping prey and slicing up the flesh are important for carnivores, like the puma and other big cats. Many animals use their tongues to obtain food. For example, flamingos use their tongues to force water from the mouth, straining out the tiny organisms on which they feed. Snails grate the surface of leaves with their rough tongues and eat the resulting mush. Anteaters and chameleons both have sticky tongues which they use to trap insects. The shape and size of a bird's beak or bill reflect the kind of food it eats. For example, hummingbirds have long beaks to extract nectar from flowers, while seed-eating birds have strong bills for cracking the shells.

Flamingo

Mosquito

Hummingbird

Bee-eater

Anteater

Wasp

Lamprey

Chameleon

Snail

THE PLANTEATERS

Green plants get their energy from sunlight through a wonderful process called photosynthesis, and they use the energy to make their own food. Animals cannot do this. They have to get their energy by eating plants or by eating animals that have already eaten plants. Without green plants there would be no life on earth.

Most of the world's animals are planteaters or herbivores. Some eat a wide range of plants, but most stick to just a few kinds. They may eat only certain parts, for which their digestive systems are well adapted. Leaves and stems consist mainly of a tough material called cellulose. This is not easy to digest, but microscopic bacteria and protozoans live in the stomachs of many plant-eating mammals and help them to digest it – after it has been crushed.

THE GIRAFFE'S JUNGLE COUSIN
The okapi was only discovered in 1901. The closest and only living relative of the giraffe, this shy animal lives in the dense tropical forests of central Africa. It feeds on leaves which it plucks from the trees with its long tongue. Its tongue can measure up to 50 cm (20 in) in length – long enough to reach up and clean its own eyes! Okapis are picky feeders. They spend time searching out certain types of leaves, tender buds and shoots, ferns, fruit and mushrooms. When they find vegetable gardens planted by human forest-dwellers, they particularly like to eat manioc and sweet potatoes.

FRESHWATER VEGETARIANS
The three species of manatee, along with their relative, the dugong, are aquatic mammals that feed almost exclusively on plants. They eat seagrasses and seaweeds. Manatees have a special adaptation: because the plants contain an abrasive substance called silica, which wears teeth down quickly, the animals shed their worn teeth throughout their lives and new ones grow in their place. Manatees live in the shallow waters and rivers around the Atlantic coasts of West Africa and tropical America.

■ MORE ABOUT OKAPIS
With its long legs and body sloping downwards from the shoulders, the okapi looks like a giraffe with a short neck. Its dark brown coat and striped legs and hindquarters help it to blend into the forest. Okapis stand about 1.6 m (5 ft 3 in) high at the shoulders and can weigh up to 230 kg (505 lb). The males have two small horns and, like giraffes, they fight for females by exchanging blows with their necks. The males stake out a territory of a few hectares. Males and females meet only at mating time. The females bring their calves up alone. The calf stays with its mother for about 12-18 months.

TREE HYRAX

Although hyraxes look like large rodents, the elephants are their nearest living relatives. Tree hyraxes live in the forests of Africa. Their padded feet with claw-like nails help them run up smooth tree trunks, and sticky secretions from glands on their feet give them even better grip. Hyraxes come out at night to munch on leaves, fruit, ferns and, sometimes, insects and birds' eggs. These noisy mammals usually live in pairs.

EUCALYPTUS FOR DINNER AGAIN!
The koala is an Australian marsupial that spends its whole life in the eucalyptus trees on which it feeds. Eucalyptus leaves contain substances that are toxic to most animals. The koala has solved this problem by developing powerful digestive juices which neutralise the poisons. Eucalyptus leaves are not very nourishing and koalas have to eat large amounts of them to obtain the energy they need to survive. They eat about 1.3 kg (3 lb) of leaves every day. Before the Australian government introduced protection laws for koalas, they were hunted extensively for their fur. Recently, disease and human encroachment on their territories have decreased numbers of koalas from several million to just a few hundred thousand. Numbers continue to dwindle.

FLOWERS AND FRUIT

Some animals have discovered that the most nourishing parts of plants are the flowers and fruits. Flowers produce dust-like pollen that triggers off seed-production when it reaches other flowers of the same kind. The pollen contains nourishing proteins and many insects and other animals find it good to eat. Many flowers attract insects by producing extra large amounts of pollen. The insects eat a lot of it, but also carry some to other flowers, where it starts the process of seed-formation. So the arrangement is useful to the plants as well as to the insects. A seed is a tiny plant surrounded by a store of food that nourishes it in the early stages of growth. Animals know that there is good food in seeds and many species, especially birds, have become specialised seed-eaters. Seeds are often protected by tough coats, but the seed-eating birds have evolved strong beaks which can open the seeds very easily. Many seeds develop inside tasty fruits that are designed to attract birds and other animals. The animals carry the fruits away to eat them and, because they scatter the seeds in different places, they help the plants to spread.

FRUIT-EATING BATS
Bats can be divided into two broad groups – fruit-eaters and insect-eaters. Fruit bats are generally larger and most species live in the tropics where fruit is plentiful throughout the year. Fruit bats help trees and plants to reproduce. The seeds pass through the fruit bat's digestive system and fall on the ground where they sprout and grow into new plants. The biggest fruit bats, with wingspans up to 2m (6 ft 6 in), are called flying foxes.

A SUCCESS STORY
Rats are the most widespread mammals on our planet. Hitching lifts on ships and other means of transport, they have followed people to the ends of the earth, settling on even the remotest islands. Rats are successful because they eat almost anything, even if they prefer seeds and fruit. Brown rat populations are made up of clans led by a dominant male with a harem of females, plus subordinate males. When there are only a few rats, they defend their territory fiercely, chasing intruders away. Large colonies are more ready to tolerate outsiders. The brown rat arrived in Europe in the 18th century, when famine pushed it west from its original home in central Asia.

THE MOCKINGBIRD'S WINTER DIET

Mockingbirds live in many parts of North America. During the spring and summer, when their young need large quantities of protein for growth, mockingbirds feed almost exclusively on insects. In winter, when insects are less plentiful, they feed on seeds and berries left on trees and bushes. Although these foods contain little protein, they contain lots of energy-rich sugars and the birds are able to survive through the cold winter months.

POWDERING ITS NOSE

South African dormice and other small rodents are among the few non-flying animals that pollinate plants. They feed on the nectar of the protea flower, a plant common in South Africa. Some species of protea produce flowers that open close to the ground and smell like rancid butter. The smell becomes stronger at night when the rodents are out and about. Attracted by this odour, some of these little animals crawl over the flowers and drink the sugary nectar that they produce. While drinking, the mice get pollen on their noses. When they pay a visit to another protea, they pollinate the plant.

■ MORE ABOUT PROTEA FLOWERS AND RODENTS

The flat-topped mountain, called Table Mountain, overlooking Cape Town in South Africa, is home to an exceptional number of plant and animal species. Table Mountain has its own cloud cover (known as the Tablecloth) which is mainly responsible for its lush vegetation. Several species of protea grow on Table Mountain; one of the most beautiful, the *Protea nana*, has brilliant red blooms. Scientists, however, were less interested in the beauty of many blooms than in some species' seemingly strange habit of growing insignificant looking flowers very close to the ground. The mystery was solved in 1978 when a biologist noticed a host of tiny paw prints near the low-growing flowers. This, and the many tunnels around the roots of the proteas, pointed to the fact that tiny rodents were feeding on the pollen produced by the flowers. This is another example of the way plant and animal species cooperate to the advantage of both. The flowers rely on the mice to move pollen from plant to plant, thus ensuring the continuation of their species, while the mice add a touch of something sweet to their diets.

NECTAR-FEEDERS

Nectar is one of the richest and most concentrated sources of food in nature. It consists almost entirely of energy-rich sugar dissolved in water. Most flowers produce it in small amounts throughout the day. At the same time, they produce strong scents that attract insects. The nectar is often produced deep down in tubular flowers, and the insects have evolved highly specialised organs to reach it. Butterflies and moths, for example, have long, slender tongues like drinking straws that can reach the bottom of the deepest flower. While probing for nectar, the insects unknowingly pick up pollen and carry it to the next flower, where it triggers off the production of seeds. Producing nectar for insects to drink thus helps the plants as well. Some hummingbirds and other birds also feed on nectar and help to pollinate the flowers.

BUSY BEES

Bees were among the first animals to be domesticated by humans, who realised the value of honey thousands of years ago. Bees feed on pollen and nectar from flowers; some of the nectar is carried to the hive by worker bees and turned into honey. When a worker bee finds a rich source of nectar she zips back to the hive and tells the other bees where it is by means of a series of rhythmic movements which scientists call the 'dance of the bees'. The German zoologist, Karl von Frisch, was the first to understand the meaning of the bee dance.

KEEPING PACE

Like some hummingbirds, butterflies and moths help to pollinate flowers and so the flower benefits from their presence. The evolution of many species of plant has gone hand in hand with that of the insects. Changes in the structure of a flower were immediately followed by changes in the structure of the butterflies and moths. An orchid in Madagascar, for example, has its nectar hidden right at the end of a 25-cm (10-in) tube and only one kind of moth is able to reach far enough inside to drink the nectar.

BATTY ABOUT NECTAR

Large tropical bats, called flying foxes, live in hot areas throughout the Old World. They eat fruit from a wide variety of plants, helping to spread the plants far and wide by scattering the seeds. One group of flying foxes are specialised nectar-feeders. They use their slender, brush-like tongues to reach deep inside the nectar-producing flowers. By unwittingly carrying pollen from plant to plant, they also help to pollinate flowers. If these bats were to become extinct, many tropical plants would also die out.

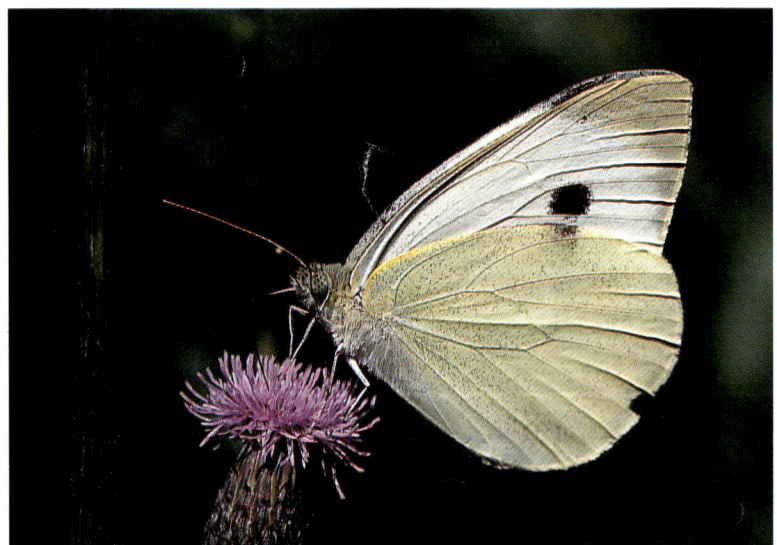

Almost all butterflies and moths have a long hollow tongue used to suck up flower nectar.

■ MORE ABOUT LORIKEETS

Lorikeets form a distinct subgroup within the parrot family. They differ from other parrots in that they mainly feed on nectar and pollen from flowering trees and shrubs. They are also called honey-parrots. Lorikeets live in Indonesia, New Guinea, Australia and the Pacific Islands. Most species are brilliantly coloured and live in large noisy groups. The males do flamboyant 'dances' to intimidate rivals and to impress females during courtship. As well as pushing their tongues into flowers to reach the nectar, they crush the flowers and lap up the juices.

SPECIALLY ADAPTED TONGUES

Compared with other birds, all parrots have large, fleshy tongues, which they use to move food around in their bills. Some species of nectar-feeding parrots have other adaptions to make them more suited to their diets. Lorikeets, or brush-tongued parrots, have a tuft of thread-like projections on the tips of their tongues. When they are resting or eating fruits or seeds they keep the tufts covered in a sheath, but when they find a flower with nectar the projections are extended into the flower to mop up the nectar.

SUSPENDED ANIMATION

Certain hummingbirds are the most specialised nectar-feeders among birds. Their beaks are very long and curved so that they can reach inside trumpet-shaped flowers. Their special way of flying, more like an insect than a bird, allows them to hover in front of a flower as they feed. The hummingbird's tongue is specially designed for drinking nectar. Although long and straw-like, it is not used to suck the nectar up but acts more like a sponge absorbing the nectar. The tongue is controlled by very long muscles stretching from the skull to the nostrils. Some hummingbirds are territorial and fiercely defend the nectar-rich plants in their area from other birds.

13

BORING FOR FOOD

Some small animals do not simply eat plants: they live most of their lives munching away right inside the plants. Animals that live like this, getting both food and shelter from the plants, are sometimes called parasites. The grubs of many tiny insects, known as leaf-miners, can live inside a single leaf. Brown patches or twisting tunnels show where they have chewed their way through the soft, nutritious tissues between the upper and lower surfaces. They bite their way out and escape when they are fully grown. The grubs of many beetles and flies and the caterpillars of several moths live inside plant stems. Some even manage to live in living and dead tree trunks, but wood is not a very nutritious substance and insects feeding on it often take several years to grow up. Some plants have evolved efficient chemical defences against grazing and tunnelling animals. Many of them contain tannins and other bitter-tasting substances, but not all planteaters are put off by them. Some actually make use of the poisons by storing them in their bodies and using them to deter their own enemies.

BARK BEETLES IN THE FORESTS
Bark beetles live under the bark of trees, in the nutritious tissue called phloem. Males and females meet up on the trunks and then bore through the bark. The female digs a little tunnel between the bark and the wood and lays her eggs in it. When the eggs hatch, the grubs make their own tunnels in the phloem. They eat it as they go and gradually spread out from the original tunnel. If the bark falls off later you can see the fascinating tunnel patterns. Each kind of beetle makes a different pattern. When they are fully grown, the grubs turn into new beetles, which chew their way out of the bark to go in search of mates and new trees. Too many bark beetles can cause serious damage to the trees.

NOISY ENOUGH TO WAKE THE DEAD
The deathwatch beetle gets its name from the ticking sound it makes in the wooden beams and furniture in which it lives. It produces this sound by striking the front part of its body, the prothorax, on the hard walls of its tunnels. Even though the insect is no more than 8 mm long (1/3 in), it makes a very loud noise which is particularly audible in the quiet of the night. According to an old superstition, the ticking sound meant that someone in the house was about to die. Scientists now know that it is a mating call. The young beetles (grubs) live in the timber for up to 5 years before growing into adults.

POPLAR BORERS

The poplar borer is a beetle whose grubs make long tunnels in the branches of poplar trees. The tunnels weaken the smaller branches, making them especially prone to wind damage. To defend themselves, the trees produce growths similar to galls (see below). In severe infestations all the smaller twigs and branches up to 15 mm (just over 1/2 in) thick develop one or more swellings. The insect larvae inside the swellings take one or two years to become adult, growing to 25 mm (1 in) in length and 8 mm (1/3 in) in diameter. Other wood-boring beetles cause damage by helping fungi to enter. The fungi cause canker, a disease that can quickly kill the trees.

THE PLANTS FIGHT BACK

Gall wasps are tiny, ant-like insects. They attack a wide range of plants, especially oaks and roses. The female gall wasps lay their eggs in buds or leaves, and when the grubs start to feed they cause the plant to swell up around them. The swellings are called galls and the gall wasp grubs feed on the nutritious tissues inside them. Fully grown grubs turn into new gall wasps and chew their way out of the galls. Each kind of gall wasp causes a different kind of gall. A robin's pincushion gall is pictured on the right. Two kinds of spangle galls are shown above. Gall-formation is the plant's way of defending itself: it stops the insects from spreading all over the plant. Shut up in their galls, the gall wasps do not do any harm to the plant.

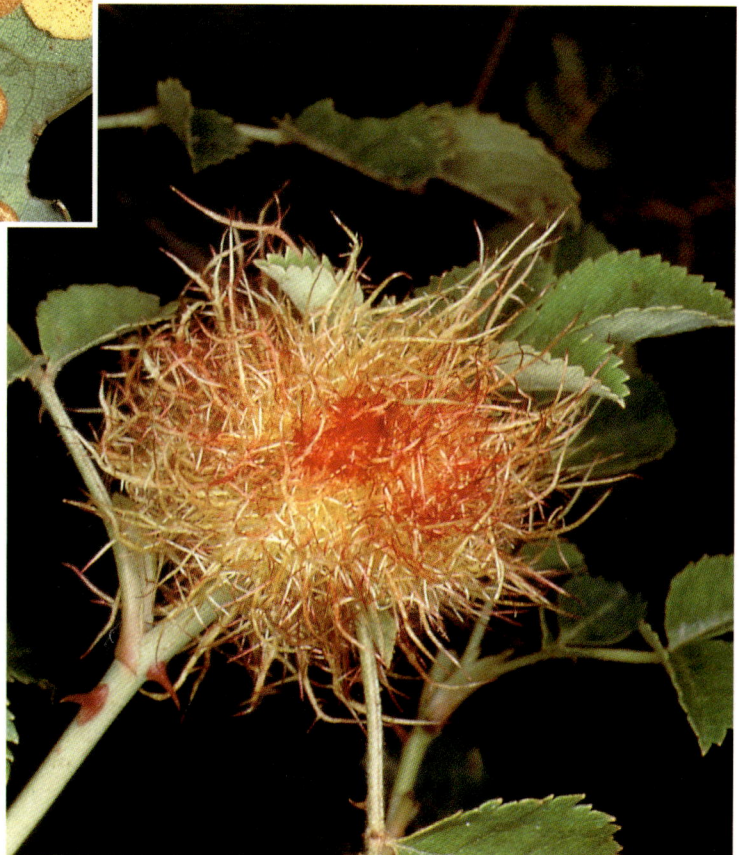

15

A DIET OF MEAT

GREAT BLUE HUNTER
The blue shark, found in seas throughout the world, is one of the fiercest predators. It can grow up to 5 m (16 ft 6 in) long and weigh more than one and a half tonnes. Like all sharks, it uses its highly developed senses to locate prey. It can detect the slightest odours in the water. Blue sharks sometimes strike seals with enough force to knock them senseless. The sharks then use their razor-sharp teeth to slice up their victims.

Meateaters or carnivores form the last links in the food chains in every ecosystem. Food chains always start with plants, because only plants can make their own food. The next link in the chain is a planteater, getting its energy from the plants that it eats. Then come one or more meateaters that get their energy by eating other animals. The final link is often a large and powerful animal, such as a shark, a wolf, or a big cat. These top predators can never be very common because there would not be enough food and energy to go round. Energy is lost at every stage of the food chain, because the animals use it up all the time. When an antelope is caught and eaten by a leopard, it contains only a small fraction of the energy that it has taken in during its lifetime. Food or energy chains are sometimes called pyramids because there are lots of plants at the base, smaller numbers of herbivores further up, and even smaller numbers of predators at the top.

GETTING A GRIP ON THINGS
The anaconda is a giant of a snake which grows to about 5 m (16 ft) long. Reports exist of specimens measuring as much as 12 m (40 ft), although there are no official records of these. Anacondas live along tropical rivers in South America. They lie in wait along river banks for prey, which they kill by constriction (squeezing them in the coils of their body until they cannot breathe). They can kill creatures as large as pigs and tapirs. They are excellent swimmers and will follow their prey into the water. This one has caught a cayman.

A DEATH STAR

Starfish are spiny-skinned animals belonging to the group called echinoderms. They are carnivores, feeding on a wide range of other animals. They also eat carrion (dead flesh). Powerful suckers under their arms help them to move and feed. The suckers can open the shells of bivalve molluscs, such as cockles and mussels. Digestive juices released by the starfish attack the muscles holding the shells shut, so the shells gradually open. The starfish then pushes its stomach into the mollusc to digest the flesh and swallow it.

The starfish closes itself around the victim, in this case a mussel.

Its suckers start to pull the shell apart. The starfish's gastric juices gradually weaken the mussel's resistance.

The mussel opens slowly. The starfish pushes part of its stomach into the shell and digests the mussel.

■ MORE ABOUT STARFISH

There are more then 1,500 species of starfish. They live in seas and oceans throughout the world, usually on coasts. The largest number of species live in the North Pacific, from Puget Sound to the Aleutian Islands. For example, Vancouver Island, off the coast of Canada, has about 70 species living in its waters that are not found elsewhere. Most starfish have five arms, although there are some with more than forty. Starfish vary in size from about 5 cm (2 in) up to 1 m (3 ft 3 in). One of the largest species inhabits the waters off the coast of the north-west of the United States.

LONE STALKER

The leopard is the most widely distributed of the big cats. It is found over most of sub-Saharan Africa, parts of North Africa and the Middle East, much of southern Asia and the Far East, as well as the snowscapes of Siberia. Leopards hunt by stalking and ambushing a wide range of prey, from small rodents to large herbivores, including antelopes and deer. Hunting usually takes place at dusk or at night, with the leopard stalking its victim for a long time before closing in for the kill. Like most of the big cats, the leopard hunts alone. Females raise their young by themselves, and hunting lessons are a basic part of cubhood.

PATIENT PREDATORS

Not all meateaters and not even all top predators are exceptionally strong or fast. They are only as big and strong as they need to be to catch their food. Many of them feed on small creatures and rely more on patience to find and capture them. Crab spiders often sit in flowers and wait for insects to arrive. The spiders are often the same colour as the flowers and the insects do not see them until it is too late: the crab spiders grab them and suck them dry. There are many other kinds of spiders, including the orb-web spiders whose silken, wheel-shaped webs are marvels of design and engineering skill. They can catch and hold insects much bigger than the spiders themselves, and the webs of some tropical spiders can even catch birds. The gladiator spiders are perhaps the most specialised of all predators. They spin sticky webs and throw them over passing insects.

POUNCING ON PREY
The North American bobcat is slightly smaller than its more widespread cousin, the lynx. Like the latter, it hunts by suddenly leaping out on its unsuspecting victims. It feeds on birds and small mammals, like snow hares. In winter, when prey is scarce, it will sometimes eat carrion.

THE GENTLE ART OF WAITING

The striped argiope spider spins a very large and extremely strong web in the grass or bushes. The females spin the largest webs. The spiders wait head-down in the centre of their web. When an insect is trapped, they race out and wrap the victim in silken thread. The prey is killed by the spider's venom, which also helps to digest the food.

■ MORE ABOUT SPIDERS

Spiders are not insects; they belong to a group of animals called arachnids which have four pairs of legs and two main body parts. They have poisonous fangs. Spiders are found on every continent except Antarctica. Over 34,000 species of spider have been described so far. They range in length from less than 1 mm (0.04 in) to about 90 mm (3.5 in). Spiders are carnivores and prey mostly on insects. Many spiders spin silken webs or threads to catch their prey, but many others, including wolf spiders and jumping spiders, chase and pounce on their victims. In most species the female is larger than the male and, unless he is careful to identify himself, the male will be mistaken for prey and eaten when he tries to mate with a female. The females lay their eggs in silken sacs. The young spiders don't look very different from their parents, except for the size.

A COLOURFUL AMBUSH

Horned frogs are among the most aggressive species of frog. These amphibians are well camouflaged by their bold patterns as they sit perfectly still in the grass or swamp water. They eat almost anything that will fit into their large mouths, from worms and insects to mice, lizards and smaller frogs. Because of the size of their mouths, which stretch almost to their legs, they are known as 'the mouth with legs'. The horned frog's bite is strong and painful because of its upper teeth. Horned frogs live in tropical America and southeast Asia.

NICE BUT FATAL

Despite their appearance, ladybirds are efficient and voracious predators. Most species feed on aphids which they find by methodically patrolling plants. They climb to the top of a shoot, and if they find no aphids they go down again and climb the next branch they meet. In this way, they cover the whole plant. The seven-spotted ladybird is the most common species. During its brief lifetime as a larva and adult, it devours more than 6,000 aphids. The larva alone eats more than 2,000 aphids. The insects' bright colouring acts as a warning to other predators who know that these tiny beetles have poisonous liquids inside.

ANYTHING GOES

Most carnivores will eat any kind of meat that comes their way. This is especially true of the smaller meat-eating mammals. They feed on other mammals, birds, reptiles, amphibians and insects. They also eat eggs and carrion – the dead bodies of other animals – and if they are really hungry, they even turn to plants. Because they take every opportunity to feed, these animals are called opportunist feeders. They are more adaptable than the bigger and more specialised meateaters and their digestive systems are less specialised. They can easily change their diet when food sources change. In autumn, for example, the opportunists often eat a lot of fallen fruit. The fox is one of the best known of the opportunist feeders. It even raids our dustbins for scraps of food. It is so good at adapting to different environments that it is just as common in towns as in the countryside. Many flesh-eating birds are also opportunist feeders.

THE AMBUSH AND STAB HUNTING TECHNIQUE
The grey heron is the largest and most widespread of the European herons. It nests from Britain to Greece, almost always close to water. It also lives in Africa and Asia. The grey heron normally stays close to marshy areas and does most of its hunting there, although it occasionally ventures into stubble fields or even further afield if it has no young to feed.
The grey heron dines on a wide variety of animals, including frogs, moles, rats and fish, which it captures with an ambush and stab technique. The heron waits, stock-still, on the banks of a lake, river or swamp until an unsuspecting victim peeks out of a hiding place. Then, with a quick darting movement of its powerful neck, it stabs its victim.

WHEREVER THE FOOD IS...
Most seagulls are highly intelligent. They take advantage of every opportunity that arises to get food. Some individuals within a species learn specialised hunting skills. For example, some gulls prey on eggs and young birds while others become specialist thieves, stealing fish from the beaks of other sea birds. Recently, seagulls have learned that where people live there will often be food. Rubbish dumps, newly ploughed fields and litter bins generally have become important sources of food. Some seagulls have learned to live in cities, sometimes even nesting there, far away from their natural habitat.

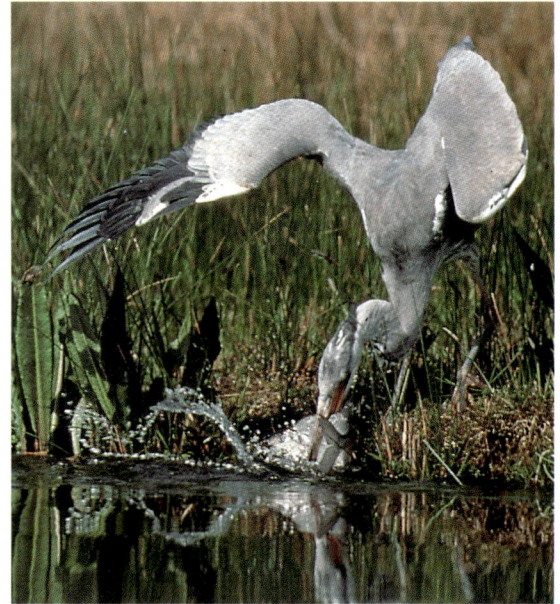

BIRD BRAIN

The raven is one of the most intelligent birds. It feeds on anything it can find, from eggs and carrion to rodents, young birds and even the placentas of mammals who have just given birth. Some scientists claim that ravens exchange information on the whereabouts of prey. Large groups of ravens often gather to feed on large carcases, and they may be joined by coyotes and other mammals.

Pick up the egg...

throw it backwards between the hind legs...

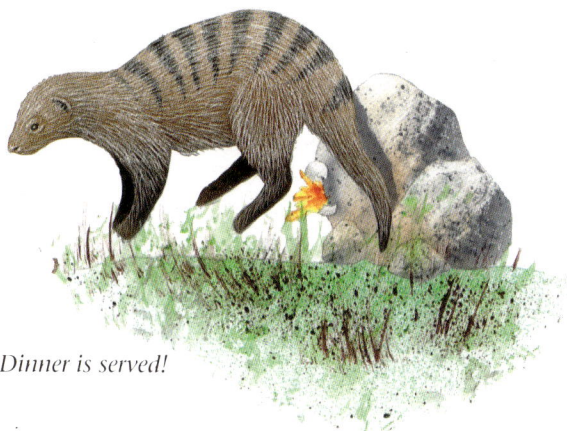

Dinner is served!

GET CRACKING!

Mongooses are active predators. They feed on small mammals, birds, reptiles, eggs and even fruit. This small opportunist predator is a cunning creature: when it wants to eat an egg, it takes the egg in its front paws and tosses it backwards between its legs against a rock to crack it open.

WILY COYOTE

The coyote is one of the most widespread carnivores in North America. Very adaptable, it will make a meal of any piece of meat it can sink its teeth into, from carrion and rodents to young deer or elk. Working together as a pack, coyotes will also attack larger animals. When no meat is available they eat vegetable matter.

■ MORE ABOUT MONGOOSES

Mongooses (or mongeese) are small carnivorous mammals with short legs, a pointed nose, small ears and a long, furry tail. There are more than 40 species living throughout Africa, Asia and southern Europe. Adult size varies considerably, ranging from 32-44 cm (12-16 in) in the dwarf mongoose to 1-1.2 m (3-4 ft) in the small-toothed mongoose. Some species live alone or in pairs while others gather together in large groups. Mongooses live in burrows and hunt during the day. Most species live on dry land, although one or two also spend some time in the water. They are bold hunters and some species will even attack and kill poisonous snakes. They are not immune to the snakes' venom and rely on speed and agility to avoid being bitten.

INSECT-EATERS

Insects are the most abundant animals on earth and they are a good source of food for many other creatures. Because insects are all rather small, the insect-eaters themselves are usually fairly small. Many small birds are specialised insect-eaters. They have superb eye-sight for spotting the insects and most have sharp, tweezer-like beaks for picking them up. Woodpeckers have powerful beaks that they use to drill into tree trunks to find wood-boring insects. Swallows and nightjars catch insects in flight by scooping them up in their gaping beaks. Bats feed in much the same way. Larger insect-eating mammals specialise in the ants and termites that live in large colonies. Large numbers of these insects can be caught at one time with very little effort. Anteaters have strong claws for ripping open the ants' nests, and long, sticky tongues that mop up the insects. Many of them also have long snouts.

A SCALY SUIT OF ARMOUR
Pangolins, or scaly anteaters, are curious creatures whose bodies are covered with hard, overlapping scales. When alarmed, they can roll into a ball, which few predators can penetrate. Four species live in Africa and three more live in southern Asia. They feed on the hordes of ants and termites that inhabit the forests and the grasslands. They use their sensitive noses to find the nests, and rip them open with their powerful claws. Their sticky tongues, which can extend up to 40 cm (16 in) in front of the mouth, pick up the insects. Pangolins have no teeth and the insects are ground up in the stomach.

THE STRANGEST MAMMAL
The aardvark is one of the strangest mammals. It lives in many parts of Africa and has no close relatives. The daily life and habits of the aardvark are also little known. It sleeps in a burrow by day and comes out at night in search of prey. It uses its strong claws to rip open ant and termite hills, and then pokes its long nose in. It mops up the insects with its long, sticky tongue. Like many other insectivores, its teeth are weak and food is 'chewed' in its muscular stomach. The aardvark swallows sand and pebbles when eating to help grind the food.

BEARDED BIRDS
The nightjar, or goatsucker, hunts only between dusk and dawn. Its mottled brown and white plumage serves as camouflage, making it almost invisible against the forest background by day. Desert-dwelling species are much lighter in colour, almost a dirty yellow, and not as spotted. The most interesting feature of all nightjars is their large gaping mouth, kept open during flight. The stiff bristles surrounding the mouth help capture the small insects on which they feed. Nightjars migrate to Africa in the autumn.

■ MORE ABOUT NIGHTJARS
There are over 80 species of nightjar spread throughout the world. They are sleek birds with large heads and tiny bills. There is little difference between males and females, except in some tropical forms where the male is more brightly coloured. Almost all nightjars are nocturnal and some biologists think that, like bats, they may use a form of echo-location to hunt more effectively in the twilight or dark. They locate prey by bouncing high frequency sounds off them and other objects.

SMELLS GOOD
The kiwi is found only in New Zealand. It cannot fly and its tiny wings are hidden in its plumage. It moves through the forests on its long muscular legs. The kiwi feeds on ants, earthworms and other small invertebrates that it finds in the ground. Its beak is similar to the long snout of many other insect-eaters. The bristles around the base serve as feelers. Its nostrils are at the tip of the beak and they help the bird to find its food. Unlike most birds, it has a good sense of smell.

23

ANIMAL PARASITES

Some animals spend all or most of their lives on or in another creature, from which they take all their food. Animals of this kind are called parasites, and the animals that they feed on are called hosts. Almost every animal is host to one or more parasitic species. Some parasites, including lice and fleas, stay on the outside of the host's body and suck blood from it. Others, such as tapeworms and roundworms, live inside their hosts and some of them have become so specialised that they are hardly recognisable as animals at all. Many live in the host's digestive system, where they soak up its food. Some parasites settle in other parts of the body, such as the eyes or the blood vessels, where they can cause serious injury. Parasites rarely kill their hosts (this would endanger their food supply), but animals with lots of parasites often die because they are too weak to escape from predators.

A MOUTH LIKE A RASP
Sea lampreys, and related freshwater species, are parasites of fish. Although they have long bodies like eels, they are more primitive vertebrates than fish; their mouths have no jaws. They feed by attaching themselves to animals, usually fish, with mouths that are like suction cups. Long horny teeth surrounding the mouth rasp away the skin and the mouth sucks up blood and other liquids from the victim. When full, the lampreys detach themselves and rest on the bottom until hunger strikes again.

RIDING ON A FISH
Many marine animals have become parasites. Crustaceans of the woodlouse group are among the most common parasites. They grip their fish or crustacean hosts, usually on their heads or backs, and bite holes in them. The parasites shown here usually live on fish that live on the sea bottom or near the coasts. They are often found on fish that live among the seaweeds. They are very common and are quite visible as they ride around on the host.

A BLOODY MEAL
Leeches are related to earthworms, although they have adopted an entirely different lifestyle. They live as parasites by sucking blood from a variety of animals. Most leeches live in water, although there are some land-living species, particularly in tropical regions. Leeches are attracted to their hosts by the heat or chemicals they emit. They attach themselves to the host, cutting the skin slightly with their three teeth; at the same time they inject a painkiller. Their saliva also contains a substance that stops the blood from clotting.

DANGEROUS GUESTS
Tapeworms are one of the best known parasites of human beings. These tapeworms spend part of their life in the stomach of a cow or a pig. Then they move into its muscles where they form hard lumps, called cysts. If a person eats this meat raw or under-cooked, the cyst develops into an adult tapeworm, attaching itself to the stomach wall by means of little hooks and suckers on its head. It absorbs food through its skin and can live for a long time in the host's body, sometimes reaching 3 m (10 ft) in length. During its stay it produces thousands of eggs which pass out of the host, ready to begin the cycle all over again.

CHARMING THIEVES

Raccoons are found practically everywhere on the American continent, from the east to the west coasts and from the mountains to the swamps of the south. They eat almost anything, from meat and plants to eggs. The raccoon is agile and intelligent. Although its diet is mainly vegetarian, it will also climb a tree to raid a bird's nest, or, like the European badger, patiently hunt for earthworms. The raccoon's slender fingers are very good at handling food and their fingertips are almost as sensitive as those of humans. No satisfactory explanation has so far been found for their habit of 'washing' their food, although some zoologists think this is done only by animals in captivity.

OMNIVORES

Many herbivorous animals occasionally eat flesh, and meateaters also eat vegetable food from time to time. Foxes, for example, enjoy fallen fruit in the autumn. But there are many other animals that regularly eat a mixture of plant and animal foods. These animals are called omnivores, which means 'eating everything'. Cockroaches, ostriches, rats, pigs, and most bears are omnivores, and so are humans and chimpanzees. The teeth and digestive systems of omnivorous creatures are less specialised than those of the carnivores and herbivores, because they have to digest both plant and animal matter. Omnivorous mammals have biting teeth at the front and chewing teeth at the back, but no big stabbing eye-teeth for killing prey, no sharp-edged cheek teeth for slicing meat, and no big grinding cheek teeth like the grazing mammals.

WHAT'S ON THE MENU TODAY?

The brown bear once lived throughout the temperate forests of Europe, Asia and North America. People have driven it out of most of its original territory. Although the bear is related to cats and dogs and other meateaters, and has fearsome teeth, its massive body is not designed for chasing and killing large animals. So, despite fierce reputations, brown bears are actually omnivores, living on varied diets of berries, roots, fruit, meat and eggs. Each subspecies has developed special skills for hunting the prey found in its territory. For example, Alaskan bears are famous for catching salmon during the spawning season when the fish swim upstream to lay their eggs.

A MOVABLE FEAST
The common crane, the only crane that nests in western Europe, is a powerful bird. During its long migrations from Africa to the woods of northern Europe, it eats everything, from potatoes in the fields of Spain to frogs in Polish swamps. Cranes always move in large groups and land only in areas where they are sure of finding food. This information seems to be handed down, from generation to generation, and the cranes always follow the same migratory routes.

MIXED DIET
The blue-tongued skink is a reptile that lives in temperate Australian forests. It can grow up to 60 cm (24 in) long. Like a few other reptiles living in colder climates, the skink does not lay eggs, but gives birth to live young. While most blue-tongued skinks are mainly vegetarian, some species (like the one shown here) eat a bit of everything, including worms, snails, insects and other invertebrates. When threatened, the skink sticks out its blue tongue to frighten the predator. It also makes its body swell to make it seem larger – a technique that many animals use.

VERSATILE TEETH
Warthogs are related to European wild boars. They both have long, continually growing canine teeth used for finding food in their native habitats. The warthog is adaptable and lives in many wooded and grassy habitats in Africa. Continually on the move, it feeds on whatever plants it can find. In dry periods it uses its tusks and tough snout to dig up the ground in search of tubers and roots. Warthogs also eat carrion and small mammals. When eating, it kneels down in a curious position, although it is always on the alert for predators, such as leopards and lions. When threatened, it often takes refuge in the dens of aardvarks, and only the long dangerous tusks are visible.

CARRION-EATERS

Whenever an animal dies there are lots of other animals queuing up to feed on the dead flesh or carrion. They range from flies and beetles to powerful vultures and hyenas. Carrion-eaters are often called scavengers, but this name is also given to animals that feed on other dead matter. Vultures and other carrion-eating birds find their food by sight, but other carrion-eaters pick up the strong smell that always surrounds dead animals. They need strong teeth or beaks to rip open the carcases, although some of the smaller scavengers, such as jackals, wait for the larger ones to finish feeding before they go in to clear up the scraps. Scavengers also need powerful digestive juices to destroy the germs that quickly invade carcases and begin the processes of decay. It all sounds a bit gruesome, but the scavengers play a very important role in breaking down and recycling the dead matter. Without them, the land would quickly be covered with dead bodies and other debris.

RAZOR-SHARP TEETH

Piranhas have earned a reputation as ferocious predators, although many species are quite small and they often prefer to feed on dead or weak creatures that are easier to catch. Piranhas are common in the rivers of eastern and central South America. They have large blunt heads with strong jaws and razor-sharp teeth that close in a scissor-like bite. Piranhas travel in groups and are attracted by the smell of blood. They usually prey on other fish and small mammals, particularly those that are weak or sick. They also eat the bodies of tiny herons and other river birds that drop out of nests overhanging the rivers. Hunting in a group, and while the mother is absent or distracted, they have been known to capture and devour baby caymans.

GRASSLAND GRAVEDIGGER

The marabou stork lives throughout most of southern Africa. It feeds mainly on dead animals, but will also capture insects, fish, rats and small birds. Marabous sometimes help themselves to carrion other scavengers are feeding on, provoking ferocious fighting between different species of scavengers. They often live near abattoirs and slaughter houses. The long naked pouch that hangs below the throat has nothing to do with food, but is used as a warning signal and during courtship.

BONE CRUSHER

With its belligerent attitude and a mouth full of sharp teeth, the Tasmanian devil looks quite savage. Yet, despite its appearance, it feeds on the carcases of dead animals it finds during its night-time wanderings. It has very powerful jaw muscles and teeth to crush the bones of carrion. Recently extinct on the Australian mainland, the Tasmanian devil is now found only in remote areas of Tasmania. It was hunted to extinction by farmers who accused it of raiding their chicken coops and who also liked its meat, which they said tasted like lamb. Like most other Australian mammals, Tasmanian devils are marsupials.

■ MORE ABOUT KING VULTURES

The king vulture is one of the most brightly coloured members of the vulture family. It has a strong, tough beak which is perfect for ripping open dead animals and pulling off their skins and feathers. Like Old World vultures (to which they are not closely related), king vultures have bald heads. This means that they can stick their heads into a bloody carcase without the problem of getting their feathers caked with blood. They have rough tongues which they use to rasp meat from carrion bones. Their claws are not particularly sharp since they are used for walking rather than for grasping prey. King vultures nest at ground level, often under a hanging rock. The incubation period lasts for about five weeks. When the young hatch they are almost completely black. Their head colours gradually develop as the birds mature.

SCAVENGING IN THE FOREST

The king vulture is the least known of the South American vultures. It lives in tropical forests, flying low over the treetops as it searches for food. Whereas most vultures and other birds find their food by sight, the king vulture probably relies on its sense of smell, because it would be difficult to spot food under the thick canopy of branches. The bird's colourful head and showy wattles probably play a role in courtship.

FEEDING ON DEBRIS

Dead plant material and animal dung lying on the ground or at the bottom of the sea or a lake is eaten and recycled by a whole range of scavenging animals. It might seem easy to obtain food when all you eat is waste plant and animal matter, but there is not usually much digestible food in this debris or detritus. This is especially true of animal droppings, because most of the useful food has already been taken out. The debris-feeders have to swallow large amounts of rubbish in order to get a small amount of food, or else they have to work hard to separate the good from the bad before swallowing it. Large animals certainly cannot get enough food and energy in this way, and most of the debris-feeding animals are insects and other small creatures. Water-dwelling debris feeders, such as cockles, pump large amounts of water through their bodies and filter food particles from it.

SEA CUCUMBERS
Sea cucumbers are echinoderms (spiny-skinned invertebrates), related to starfish and sea urchins, whose body has evolved into the shape of a long sausage. They live on the sea bed, feeding on detritus. They use feathery tentacles around their mouths to stir up the sand which they swallow. Any nourishing particles are digested. Many sea cucumbers stay buried in the sea bed with only their tentacles showing. The feathery branches act like a net to trap particles of food. This one has fired out some sticky threads, which protect it from some of its enemies.

A DIET OF DUNG
Scarabs are large dung beetles found in many of the warmer parts of the world. They feed mainly on herbivore dung, which is rich in vegetable matter. The beetles eat it themselves and use it to nurture their larvae. After digging a hole in the dung, the beetles lay a few eggs. When the larvae hatch, they find themselves in a safe 'room' made of food in which they can feed and grow. In this way, dung beetles recycle undigested vegetable matter left by herbivores. They also return vital nutrients, such as nitrogen, to the soil where plants can use them to grow. Many scarabs bury the dung balls, after rolling them to suitable spots. They sometimes use carnivore dung as well.

SLOW BUT DANGEROUS
Millipedes are common invertebrates living in soil and plant debris all over the world. Their body structure is fairly primitive but they have large numbers of slender legs. They feed on plant and animal detritus. The structure of their mouth is quite simple; glandular secretions help them soften vegetable matter before eating it. In some tropical species the mouth has been transformed into a kind of beak, used to pierce plant walls and suck out the sap.
Although slow, millipedes are often dangerous. Many have glands that produce poisonous or irritating substances. Some tropical millipedes can spray these substances up to 30 cm (12 in). Fortunately their bright colours warn other animals to keep away.

TINY FARMERS
Earthworms are very important for the well-being of the soil. These small segmented worms swallow soil as they tunnel and extract the nutritious particles. Undigested soil is passed out of the body and deposited as worm casts on or near the soil surface. This has a beneficial effect on the soil because the lower layers of soil are brought to the surface and the top layers of organic waste sink into the soil where they can be completely decomposed by bacteria. Earthworm tunnels are very long and sometimes go down as much as 1 m (3 ft), especially in very dry or very cold weather.

FILTER-FEEDERS

Oceans, lakes and ponds contain millions of tiny floating plants and animals, collectively known as plankton. They are sometimes so abundant that the water becomes cloudy – almost like soup. Lots of other animals feed by filtering the nutritious plankton from the water. A big whale swallows about 2 tonnes of it every day. Barnacles comb the little animals from the water with their feathery legs, while many other creatures suck in currents of water and strain the plankton from it.

KNEE DEEP IN LUNCH
Although large, flamingos feed on tiny crustaceans in lakes and lagoons. Their filtering system resembles that of whales (though on a smaller scale). Water is sucked into the mouth where a large muscular tongue pumps it through a kind of sieve lining the beak. The tiny crustaceans are held back and swallowed. In the two Old World species, the greater flamingo and the lesser flamingo, the filter plates differ in size so that they sieve out different prey, thus eliminating competition between the species.

OUR MARINE ANCESTORS
Sea squirts look like small cylindrical bags with two openings. They draw water in through one opening, filter food particles out and then discharge it through the other. Most sea squirts live permanently fixed to the sea bed. Their structure is so simple it is hard to believe that sea squirts are distant relatives of vertebrates.

UNDERWATER LACE
Sea fans are simple sea animals although they look more like plants. They live in flexible tubes. Two feathery gills extend from the top of the tube. They capture tiny particles of food as they float by on the ocean currents.

Humpback and other baleen whales strain plankton out of the water using the baleen plates that grow down from either side of the roof of their mouth. The whale opens its mouth wide, engulfing the plankton and large amounts of water. The water is then sieved through the baleen plates, separating the plankton which is then swallowed.

GENTLE GIANTS

The humpback whale is one of the largest animals on our planet even though it feeds on tiny crustaceans which it finds in the cool Arctic and Antarctic seas. Humpback whales concentrate in areas where there is an abundance of 'krill' which is their major food.

MICROSCOPIC SEA DWELLERS

Under certain conditions some areas of the ocean are suddenly invaded by abundant growths of microscopic plants. This sets off a long and complicated food chain and within just a few days there is an explosion of zooplankton which eat the plants by filtering them through their gills or by other means. Zooplankton (right) are small animals that are carried along on ocean currents. The smaller ones are eaten by the larger ones, such as the shrimp-like creature called krill (above). These are eaten by fish and other larger animals.

HUNTERS AND AMBUSHERS

Whether they eat meat or plants, all animals must develop special senses and techniques for recognising and gathering or catching food. As we have already seen, meateaters capture their prey in two main ways – either by chasing it or by ambushing it. Hunters that chase their prey over long distances have muscles that can go on working for long periods without getting tired, but they cannot sprint at high speed. Cheetahs can sprint at high speed, but only for short distances. Mammals that lie in wait for their prey and ambush it are often heavier than the hunters. They leap on to their prey and kill it with the impact of their bodies as much as by biting it or using their claws. Ambushing spiders and insects also tend to be heavier than the hunters. The praying mantis, for example, has large, spiky front legs which it snaps around its victims. Many ambushers lure their victims within range with colourful fins or other bits of their bodies that act as bait.

MONARCH OF THE FOREST
The tiger is the largest of the big cats. The Siberian tiger can weigh up to half a tonne. Tigers live mainly in areas of long grass, where they can stalk and ambush all kinds of animals, from large antelopes to small deer. Their striped coats, which blend in perfectly with the dappled patterns of shade and light, and their stealthy movements allow them to approach their prey unseen. As with other highly evolved predators, tigers have developed different hunting methods according to their environment and their prey. For example, in Ranthambore Park in India, tigers have learnt to attack sambar deer while they are in the water and cannot move fast. In Siberia, tigers chase deer into deep snow where they sink and cannot escape.

ANGLER FISH
There are many weird and wonderful creatures in the ocean depths! Many angler fish, like this one, have a luminous lure on their head. It acts as a bait to attract the fish they like to eat.

A SUPERB FISHERMAN
The osprey circles over lakes and rivers at heights up to 30 m (98 ft), using its sharp eyes to look for fish under the surface. Then it plunges down, entering the water feet first with a great splash, and grabbing the fish before it can escape. The bird sometimes goes right under the water, but quickly rises again with its prey. Its feet are equipped with small nodules that help it to grip the slippery fish as it carries it away.

THE JAWS OF DEATH
At first sight, adult ant lions look a bit like dragonflies, although their antennae and wings are different. But the young stages of the two insects are very different. As soon as it hatches, a young ant lion digs a funnel-shaped hole in sandy soil. It then hides at the bottom and waits. It throws sand at ants and other small insects that stumble into the hole, and they slide down the sides, right into the ant lion's waiting jaws.

WEAPONS AND TECHNIQUES

Capturing prey is not simply a question of having strong muscles or bursts of speed: hunters also need good senses and perfect co-ordination between the senses and the muscles. Ambushers need good co-ordination as well if they are to grab their victims at just the right time. The predators also have to kill their prey, and they have evolved just the right weapons to do it. Cats and dogs have large, stabbing teeth; birds of prey have sharp talons; and spiders and many snakes have their venom. These features were not originally used for killing, but they have been modified during millions of years of evolution and are now deadly weapons. Insects and other invertebrate predators do not have to learn how to hunt or catch food, and spiders never need lessons in web-making. They are born with the necessary hunting skills or techniques already implanted in their brains and automatically know what to do. Behaviour of this kind is called instinctive behaviour. It is different among the hunting mammals, however. These youngsters have to learn by watching their parents, and they perfect their techniques with months or even years of practice in the family.

LOOKING BEFORE IT LEAPS
The kingfisher is the most colourful of European birds. Despite its bright colouring, it is not easy to spot when perched on a branch above a stream waiting for prey. The kingfisher feeds on small fish which it captures by diving into the water from above. Often, just before it dives, it hovers in the air beating its wings rapidly. When it hits the water its eyes are covered by a protective membrane and it can't see, so before it takes the plunge it has to be absolutely sure of the position of its prey.

■ MORE ABOUT COBRAS
Cobras are all highly venomous snakes that can expand their neck ribs to create a hood. They live in the warm areas of Asia, Africa and Australia. The family includes the longest poisonous snake in the world – the king cobra of India – which can measure up to 5.5 m (18 ft) in length. Cobras feed mainly on frogs, smaller snakes, rodents and other vertebrates. Most species lay eggs which hatch into young, although a few species bear live young.

BIRD-EATING SPIDERS

Bird-eating spiders live in the warmer parts of America. Although many look alarming because of their size, their venom is not harmful to humans. Instead of spinning webs and lying in wait for prey, most species wander along the floor of tropical forests or climb trees actively hunting for birds and small mammals. Others dig burrows, line the walls with silk and then wait for prey. If handled, the bird-eating spider defends itself by shedding its abdominal hair, which acts as an irritant and can cause severe swelling.

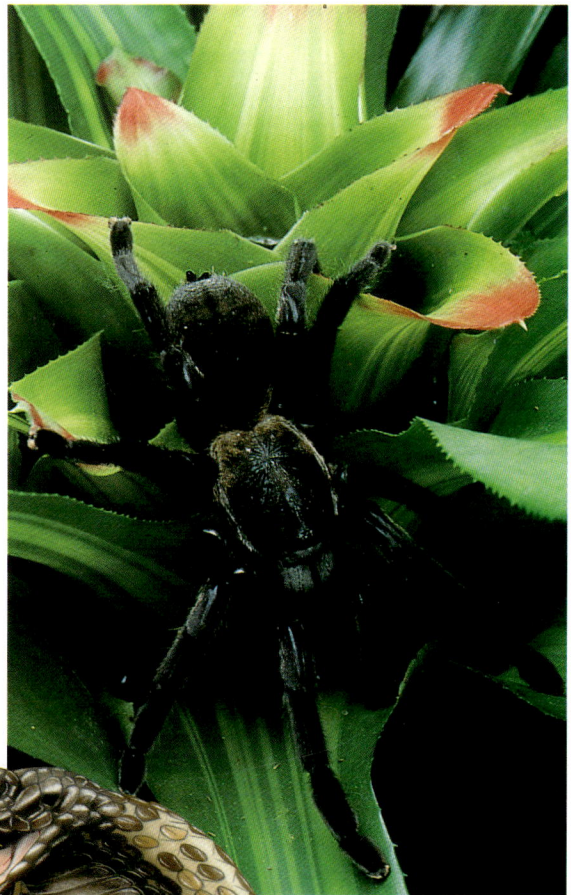

GOLDEN HUNTER

The golden eagle is one of the largest birds of prey in the northern hemisphere. It lives in the mountains and rugged areas of Europe, Asia and North America. It can fly very fast when chasing prey and quite slowly when scouting an area. The eagle adopts different hunting strategies depending on season, prey and terrain. In the European Alps, for example, where the marmot is its preferred food, the eagle flies along at ground level in order to approach the rodents without being seen by their lookout. In other areas eagles feed on prey like snow hares or partridge which they pursue and capture at high speed. Eagles have been known to chase young chamois or mouflon goats over cliffs and to pick up their bodies at the bottom.

RAINING VENOM

The spitting cobra lives in Africa. Like other members of the cobra family, its venom is highly poisonous. It is potent enough to kill large animals, including people. The spitting cobra's teeth, which act as syringe-like containers for the venom, have holes at the front, allowing the snake to squirt its poison over long distances. It uses its venom both to attack prey and to defend itself. When hunting, the venom quickly kills prey such as birds, mammals or other snakes. For defence, the snake squirts it into the eyes of attackers up to several metres away, and this can cause blindness. As in all snakes the venom is a modified kind of saliva.

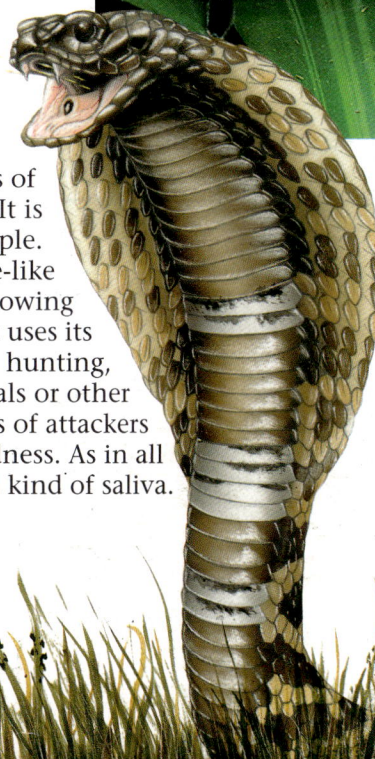

STOCKING THE LARDER

Food is not always readily available and many animals have learned to store some away for use in times of scarcity. Bears, dormice and other animals that sleep for long periods in the winter usually feed up and put on weight in the autumn. Their bodies gradually use up the food reserves during the winter months. But storing extra fat in the body can slow animals down and make them easier to catch, so species that remain active in the winter usually store their food somewhere else. Squirrels and other animals that feed on seasonal nuts and seeds store them up when they are in season and gradually eat them in the winter. The larder has to be close to home, but also has to be hidden from other animals that might steal the food. Many squirrels bury their stores in the ground or hide them in hollow trees. Foxes and other predators even store meat for a while, especially in snowy places: buried in the snow, the meat keeps well – just like in a freezer.

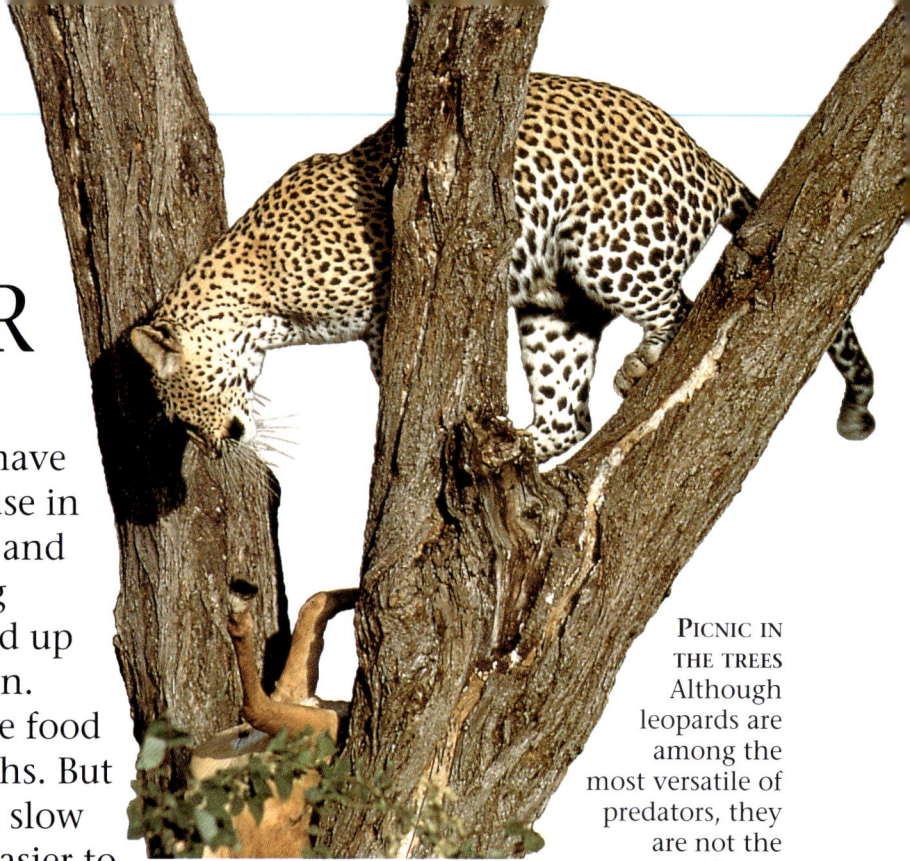

PICNIC IN THE TREES Although leopards are among the most versatile of predators, they are not the strongest. African leopards have to contend with hyenas and lions trying to steal their food. To protect their catch from theft, leopards often drag it up into a tree where they can eat undisturbed. Using their powerful jaws they can lift even quite heavy carcases, including those of small zebras and gazelles. Keeping the meat in a tree also seems to discourage vultures which have trouble finding it in the branches. Asian leopards are less likely to eat in the treetops because there are no lions or hyenas to threaten them.

BUTCHER BIRDS
The great grey shrike lives in Europe, North Africa and North America. Although they are quite small birds (slightly smaller than a thrush), pairs defend extensive territories, sometimes as large as 40 hectares (96 acres), in which they mate and hunt for food. Although great grey shrikes are 'songbirds' they share the hunting instinct and beak structure of birds of prey. They feed on small mammals, birds, lizards and insects. When food is plentiful they use special storerooms in thorn bushes. The prey is hung on the thorns and taken down to be eaten when required. This habit has earned the birds in this species the nickname of 'butcher birds'.

■ MORE ABOUT WOODPECKERS
There are almost 200 species of woodpecker throughout the world. They are distinctive birds, usually with small-to-medium sized, sturdy bodies and strong, sharp beaks. Most woodpeckers spend their whole lives in the trees. In the mating season many males use their beaks to tap out communication signals on hollow trunks and branches. Most species feed on insects which they pick out from under the bark of trees with their pointed beaks. They help control numbers of bark and wood boring insects, which might otherwise damage the trees. Many species dig nesting holes in tree trunks to create dwellings for rearing their young.

DESIGNER STOREROOMS
The American acorn woodpecker lives in groups of 3 to 12 individuals in deciduous woodlands from the north-west of the United States to Colombia. The birds in each group are usually part of the same family. They defend a territory of around 5 hectares (12.4 acres), in which they mate and hunt for food. When they find acorns or other nuts, or even insects that they can't eat immediately they store them in dozens of small holes drilled in trees, telegraph poles or buildings. The acorns are well-hidden and only another woodpecker from the group can take them out because the storeroom is one of the most protected areas in their territory.

UNDERGROUND STOREROOMS
Moles dig very long underground tunnels for shelter and to search for their favourite foods, such as earthworms and other invertebrates. The tunnels themselves act as a kind of trap; worms breaking into a tunnel are easily caught and eaten by the moles. When it is necessary to store food, such as before autumn and winter, the mole decapitates the earthworms and stores them in a special chamber. The largest store of earthworms ever found contained 1,200!

WATERING HOLES

The African savanna is hot and dry for most of the time. Rain falls for a few weeks each year and fills the rivers, but then the long dry season starts and water becomes harder and harder to find. The lakes and rivers shrink and only scattered watering holes are left. These draw animals from near and far like magnets. The first to arrive are those that need to drink most often – the antelopes and zebras. Giraffes and rhinoceroses are less affected by the drought at first because they eat lots of juicy green leaves. They usually come to the water holes later in the dry season. The animals drop lots of dung, which attracts hordes of insects to the water holes; and the insects attract lots of birds.

FIRST IN LINE
Wildebeest and other antelopes, among the most common savanna animals, travel towards the watering holes in long dusty lines spread out across the savanna.

ELEPHANT-MADE HOLES
Sometimes the watering holes are made by elephants digging for underground water which they can smell with their sensitive trunks. These pools soon fill up with mud and the elephant's excrement, but they are safer than most holes because there are no crocodiles or other predators lurking beneath the surface.

PINK LAKES
Some African lakes have high levels of salt, soda and magnesium deposits. Only a few species of crustaceans and the animals that feed on them, like flamingos, can survive in these conditions. The pink pigments of the crustaceans cause the flamingos' feathers to become pink. Many of these lakes (Natron, Kivu and others) are ideal breeding grounds for flamingos because they can bring up their young protected from predators by the salty waters. Thousands of birds breed on these lakes.

IN SEARCH OF FISH
As the rivers and lakes dry up, the few fish left find themselves flapping around in just a few centimetres of water. At this point predators like these pelicans arrive. They work the waters until not a single fish is left. When the water is completely dry they fly off to another shrinking watering hole.

FIRST IN, FIRST SERVED
The order of arrival determines who drinks first, though some larger and stronger animals jump the queue and smaller herbivores like antelopes and gazelles have to wait for a free space to dip their noses in. The warthogs, seen here at the front of the picture, have had to make do with the murky, muddy water left by the zebras, although they don't seem to mind.

THE IMPORTANCE OF WATER

Food cannot be digested and used in the body without water. All the other processes that go on inside the body also require water. It is used to carry away waste materials, and in mammals it also helps to control the body temperature through sweating. Meateaters get some water from the animal flesh that they eat, and plant sap provides some for herbivores, but the animals need to drink as well. Water is particularly important for new-born animals. Baby mammals get water in the milk that they drink, and most baby birds get water in the juicy insects that their parents bring them. Desert-living sandgrouse travel many kilometres to find water for their nestlings and carry it back in their sponge-like feathers. Very few animals can survive for more than a few days without drinking, but there are some beetles and scorpions that never drink. They conserve water very carefully in their bodies, so they can make do with the small amounts that they get from their food.

EGG WATERING

The shoebill, also known as the whale-headed stork, is a large wading bird. It lives in some of the vast marshlands of central Africa. Its large bill is used as a shock absorber while hunting, when it launches its entire weight against the reeds as it plunges after fish, small crocodiles, amphibians and other animals. It also uses its beak to carry water to keep its eggs and hatchlings cool during the hot African summer. The eggs are watered four or five times a day and, when they hatch, so are the chicks. As they grow, the young birds learn to drink the water in which their parents bathe them.

■ MORE ABOUT STORKS

Storks are large wading birds with long legs and long beaks. They live in many parts of the world, although the largest number of species live in Africa and Asia. Storks have long, broad wings and are excellent fliers. Unlike most birds which feed by sight (first observing prey, then grabbing it with their beaks), many storks use another strategy, called feeding by touch. This involves keeping the bill open in the water and snapping it shut when something touches it. This method is effective when hunting at night or in muddy swamp waters, or where underwater vegetation is dense. Touch-feeding requires sensitive receptors on the horny bill covering and lightning reflexes.

BATHTIME!
Cormorants are aquatic birds widespread on seacoasts and inland water systems throughout the world. The great cormorant of Europe and Asia is the largest of the species. It nests on rocky ridges or in treetops. Since the young cormorants are unable to get water themselves, their parents bring it to them. The parent birds carry the water in their gullets and literally shower their young to cool them down. When the hatchlings need to drink, the parents open their beaks and let the water run into the young birds' throats.

DUNE CATS
The sand cat, of the Sahara and the deserts of the Arabian peninsula, never drinks water. It is able to survive because it gets the moisture it needs from the blood of the animals it hunts and kills. It feeds mainly on rodents and other small mammals which live at the bottom of the dunes where plant wastes are carried by the wind. The sand cat also eats scorpions, reptiles and insects. Together with the fennec fox and the Saharan leopard, it is one of the few carnivorous mammals that manage to survive in the barren desert environment.

WATER OFF A BEETLE'S BACK
Some species of darkling beetle in the Namib Desert have discovered a perfect way of gleaning water from the desert air. When the water level in its body gets low, the beetle raises its rear against the wind. The Namib Desert is very dry and the only moisture available is in the dense fog which rolls in from the sea in the early mornings. The mist in the air condenses on the beetle's rear and runs down its back and into its mouth. Scientists have found that these beetles can increase the level of water in their bodies by 34 per cent using this method. In human terms, this would be the equivalent of a man weighing 70 kg (11 stone) drinking 24 litres (5 gallons) of water!

TO THE ENDS OF THE EARTH AND BACK! The Arctic tern breeds in the far north (sometimes within the Arctic circle), where it feeds by snatching fish from the surface of the sea in a series of rapid dives. When the mating season is over, the tern flies to the other side of the world to spend the northern winter on the pack ice just north of the Antarctic circle. Here it uses the same hunting techniques as in the north, feeding on small fish that swim close to the surface. This small bird covers some 32,000 km (20,000 miles) each year. By passing from the Arctic summer to the Antarctic summer, it enjoys more hours of daylight than any other animal.

VANISHED MIGRATION
The springbok is one species that has paid dearly for human development. During the 19th century, the arid interior of southern Africa was home to millions of springbok. In times of drought, when the grass had all but disappeared, the antelopes would set off in search of food and water. They sometimes covered great distances but when European settlers started to farm the land things changed. The settlers stopped the springbok from crossing their lands, and ended the great migratory movements. There are now far fewer springbok in Africa.

MIGRATING FOR FOOD

Migration is one of the most extraordinary events in nature. Huge flocks or herds of animals set off together on journeys that sometimes cover hundreds or even thousands of kilometres. The animals usually move when seasonal changes affect their food supplies. For example, during the dry season the grass becomes dry and inedible in many parts of Africa, and the wildebeest and zebras walk hundreds of kilometres to new grazing lands. Later in the year they move back again. But not all migrations are so spectacular: many mountain animals just move a few hundred metres down the mountainsides in the autumn and up again in the spring. When a population becomes too big for the local food supply, many of the animals are forced to move to new areas, but in these instances they do not return. These movements, well known in lemmings and locusts, are called emigrations.

FLIGHT OF THE BUTTERFLIES

During the summer monarch butterfly larvae feed on the poisonous leaves of the milkweed plant in Canada and the United States. The caterpillars become poisonous themselves and the poisons are carried over to the adults. In autumn, the adult butterflies fly south. They fly north again in spring, the females laying eggs along the way.

MIGRATION ON THE STEPPES OF CENTRAL ASIA

The saiga is a kind of antelope with a strange, swollen snout that has inhabited the steppes of central Asia for 20,000 years. Only the male saiga have horns which they use to fight each other during the mating season. Each male takes between 5-15 mates which it defends from other males. In winter, when the northern landscape is covered by snow and freezing winds blow, thousands of saiga head south to better grazing lands. In spring they move north again. They are closely observed by a number of other species as they move; eagles try to catch young saiga that lag behind and wolves wait to eat the placentas of the females after they have given birth.

■ MORE ABOUT SAIGA

During the last ice age the saiga inhabited a vast area between Britain and eastern Siberia. It is now confined to the steppes of central Asia. Up until a few years ago, the saiga was faced with extinction, its numbers reduced to just a few thousand. A very successful campaign to protect the animals has allowed numbers to increase and the seasonal migrations to continue. The saiga are well adapted to their environment; their fine-boned legs and split hooves allow them to move at speed over the snow-covered steppes. The adult saiga stands about 75 cm (30 in) at the shoulder. Its coat is short and pale brown in summer and thick and light-coloured in winter.

USING TOOLS

Animals have always competed with each other for food, and evolution has produced many amazing adaptations designed to increase the animals' ability to find and catch food. Various parts of their bodies have become altered or adapted as each species has become specialised for catching and dealing with particular kinds of food. Changes in behaviour have also been very important: some have enabled animals to move into different habitats and to feed on different kinds of food, while others have enabled them to obtain their food more efficiently. There are some really astonishing hunting strategies in the animal world, but among the most surprising is the use of tools in finding and capturing food. It was once thought that human beings were the only animals that used tools, but scientists have now discovered quite a lot of tool-using animals.

FISHING FOR MOTHS
Not all spiders build big complicated webs to trap their prey. Some make do with just one sticky, silken thread. The bolas spiders are among the most skilful single-thread hunters. They live in many parts of the world, but the best-known species comes from Australia. This red-and-cream predator positions itself on a plant stem and releases a length of silk with one or more drops of glue-like substance on it. When it detects a moth or some other likely victim it whirls the thread vigorously around in an attempt to hit the prey. If it does, the gluey thread sticks to the prey's body and the spider reels it in to eat. It seems that the spider also perfumes its 'fishing rod' with the smell of female moths, so the males come close to investigate.

DARWIN'S WOODPECKER FINCH
Darwin's woodpecker finch is one of several finch species descended from the few birds that colonised the remote Galapagos Islands thousands of years ago. The original birds adapted to their new environments by learning, among other things, to eat different foods from the ones they were used to on the mainland. Normally these birds feed on insects in rotting wood, and on the Galapagos one of them learned to use cactus spines, twigs or small leaves to drive insects out of the wood.

PRECISION STONES

The sea otters that live along the Pacific coast of North America are famous for their use of a tool. When they pick up a large shellfish or sea urchin from the sea floor, they open the shell, usually while floating on their backs, by banging it against a stone held on their chests. Some otters even carry these stones around with them.

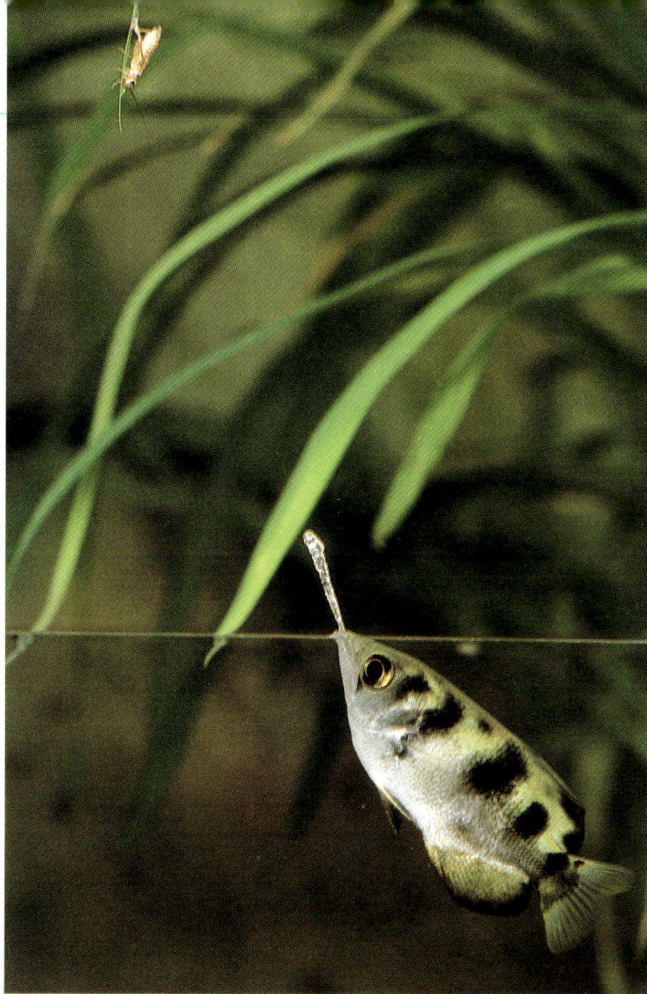

PRECISION FISHING

The archer fish lives in the mangroves of south-east Asia. Mangrove swamps are labyrinths of tree roots and debris washed up twice a day by the tide. They are home to thousands of animals, particularly insects that come to hide from predators at high tide. The archer fish has discovered a way of, quite literally, knocking insects out of the trees and into its mouth. The fish has a specially adapted mouth from which it squirts water at the insects with great precision. Its grey/green colour and flat back allow it to blend in with its surroundings, making it hard for the insects to see from above.

BETRAYAL IN THE SHADE

The black heron lives in Africa, hunting for prey in swamps and ponds. It feeds on small fish, mammals and aquatic reptiles which it hooks out of the water with a quick flick of its neck and deadly beak. Its most curious behaviour is not at the moment of capture but in preparing for the catch. The small heron moves slowly through the water with one or both wings raised, casting a shadow and preventing reflection. In this way it not only gets a better view into the water but also creates a shady place where fish instinctively feel safer. Attracted by the shade, the fish are easy prey for the heron.

DAILY FOOD

THE BIGGEST APPETITE
In the first 56 days of its life the caterpillar of the polyphemus moth of North America eats food weighing 86,000 times its own birthweight!

PICKY TICK
The castor-bean tick is a hard-backed member of the arachnid group. It is an animal parasite that feeds on the blood of sheep. While feeding, the tick can take in an enormous volume of blood for such a small animal. It does this by expanding its abdomen to double its normal size.

The amount of food eaten in a day depends on a variety of factors. Some foods have more nutritional value than others and animals need less of these foods. In the breeding season, female mammals need more food than usual because they have to nourish the babies inside them. And when the babies are born the mothers need extra food to produce their milk. Some birds change their diets from season to season, often eating buds in early spring, caterpillars in late spring and summer, and seeds in the autumn. Hibernating mammals eat nothing during the winter, although they prepare themselves by feeding well and putting on weight in the autumn. Many insects eat only when they are young. Caterpillars, for example, spend almost all their time eating and growing, but when they turn into moths many of them stop eating: they devote all their energies to mating and laying eggs. The digestive system of a species determines its diet. A carnivore cannot become a herbivore because its digestive juices are designed for breaking down meat.

A MEATEATER TURNED VEGETARIAN

The evolution of the giant panda is one of the most interesting and extraordinary among all mammals. The panda is related to the bear family and like the bear it has a carnivore's (or omnivore's) digestive system. The intestine is quite short, because flesh is easy to digest and carnivores do not need a long digestive system. However, for some unknown reason, the panda is a herbivore and feeds mainly on bamboo shoots. But it does not digest the bamboo very well and, because the plants have a much lower protein content than meat has, the panda has to eat a great deal. It manages to extract just enough energy from the bamboo to stay alive. Pandas occasionally eat insects and rodents. Some zoologists claim that when food is scarce they will eat livestock, such as sheep, thus reverting back to their carnivorous nature.

THE COMMON GOOD

Lions are the only big cats that live together in groups in which the individual's behaviour is organised and attuned to the needs of the others and the pride as a whole. The pride, centred on several closely related females, stays together permanently, defending its territory from other groups. The group organisation can be seen very clearly during hunting. Although some zoologists deny that there is any coordinated action, most people who have seen a group of lionesses hunting will agree that they are working together. A few lions will chase the prey (an antelope, zebra, wildebeest or some other animal) towards the others who lie in wait in the long grass. They leap out and kill the animal when it gets near them. In this way even large animals, like giraffes or buffaloes, can be caught.

UNGENTLE GIANTS

The black rhinoceros is one of the largest animals of the African savanna. Its bulk, dangerous horn and furious temper make it difficult for carnivores, even groups of lions, to capture. Using its long, flexible upper lip, it feeds on twigs and leaves of shrubs and trees, including the thorny branches of the acacia tree, which it breaks off with its horn. The black rhino is able to recognise the nutritional value of certain plants and carefully searches them out. The white rhinoceros has a broad, flat snout designed for grazing. Because the two species eat different foods they do not compete and live together in harmony. Excessive hunting has led to the near extinction of both species.

ON THE SHOULDERS OF GIANTS

Oxpeckers are small birds that spend most of their lives riding on large herbivores. They hold on with strong claws and use their beaks to pick off parasites and dead skin. Sometimes oxpeckers warn herbivores of danger by squawking or flying away. Oxpeckers are an example of how two or more species can benefit each other by living in close proximity. This is called symbiosis.

FOOD FOR ALL

Animals do not live in isolation; they are all part of a vast web or mosaic in which every kind of plant and animal plays its part. In the search for food, for example, animals can be helped or hindered by plants, by other animals, or by non-living environmental factors such as ice and snow. We have already seen how plants defend themselves against herbivores, and how herbivores protect themselves from carnivores: these are examples of how animals can be hindered in their search for food. A more subtle, but very important factor comes into play when two or more species compete for the same food. When this happens, either the weaker species die out or move away or the different species 'reach an agreement' and share out the food resources so that there is enough food for them all. Such a division of resources leads to specialised feeding habits, often with behavioural changes and sometimes physical changes as well. Many examples can be seen on the African savanna.

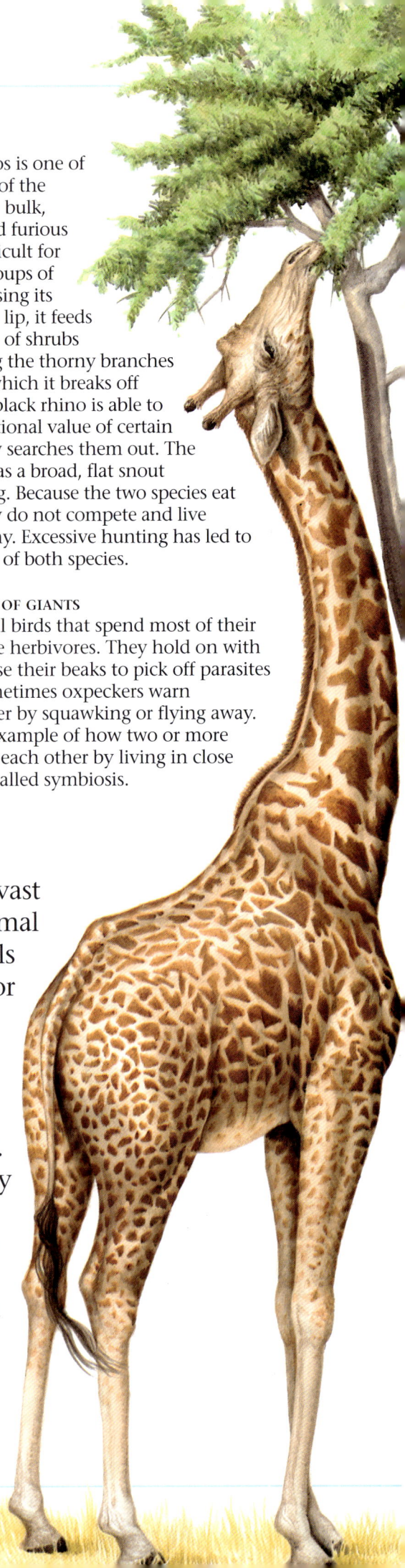

◼ MORE ABOUT GIRAFFES

Giraffes are the tallest animals on earth. Males can grow as high as 5.8 m (19 ft). Their long, flexible necks are useful for finding food that other animals can't reach; giraffes also use them to gain extra momentum and speed when running. By swinging them back and forth, they can reach speeds of up to 55 km/h (35 mph). The giraffe's neck is often cited as the textbook example of evolutionary adaptation. Because a long neck gives them access to food out of reach of other animals, giraffes born with long necks have been more successful breeders and have, very gradually, replaced ones with shorter necks.

STANDING TALL

The gerenuk is a slender, long-necked gazelle from east Africa. Although shorter than a giraffe's neck, the gerenuk's is long enough to give it an edge on other animals when feeding, for example, on the acacia tree. It reaches even higher by rearing up on its hind legs and pulling branches towards itself with its front legs. Unlike the giraffe, which needs to drink at least once a week, the gerenuk can go much longer without water. This means it can live in places that are too dry for many other grazing animals to survive.

FEEDING AT THE TOP

Giraffes eat a wide variety of plants and for this reason have spread throughout many regions of Africa. The acacia tree is the giraffe's favourite food. Even the tree's sharp thorns are not enough to discourage the giraffe from nibbling at its tender topmost leaves. Giraffes have no competitors for their main source of food because no other animal can reach it. They wrap their long tongues, measuring up to 45 cm (18 in) in length, around the twigs, softening the tough leaves with saliva before plucking them off. Giraffes also eat fruits, shoots and seeds.

PESTS AND GUESTS

Many animals live in close contact with humans, taking advantage of the shelter we provide in our homes and the wide variety of foods that we eat. Most of these animals are omnivores and they make use of every single scrap of food that we leave behind, as well as taking unused food from shelves and cupboards. Some household insects even thrive on things that are completely inedible to us, such as woollen clothing, furniture and the glue that holds books and cartons together. Animals have travelled all over the world with people, and many have adapted very well to their new homes – sometimes too well. Rats carried on ships to some of the Pacific islands completely wiped out several species of birds and other animals that originally lived there.

A DANGEROUS BUZZ
Mosquitoes are among the least well-loved of our companions, mainly because they feed on us! Only the female mosquito's mouth is equipped with the necessary piercing and sucking tools. She has six pointed needles that fit together to form a slender tube like a hypodermic needle. When the mosquito bites, its saliva enters the wound immediately to prevent the blood from clotting. Not all mosquitoes attack people; most species feed on other animals, including amphibians, reptiles and birds.

A CLOSE COMPANION
The house mouse has always lived alongside people, feeding on the things that we store or discard. It lives in houses, shops, bars and mills, but can also survive outdoors in hedges and fields. The mouse is a nocturnal animal, and only ventures out to feed at night. It eats stored foods, such as seeds, grain, and preserved foods in general. It eats only the small amount it needs to maintain itself, but its droppings contaminate vast stocks of food stored for human consumption. Outside, it feeds mainly on insects and seeds and is itself eaten by owls, cats, foxes and many other predators. Food also determines the social life of the mouse. Mice with plentiful food supplies form stable groups, while others form smaller and less stable families.

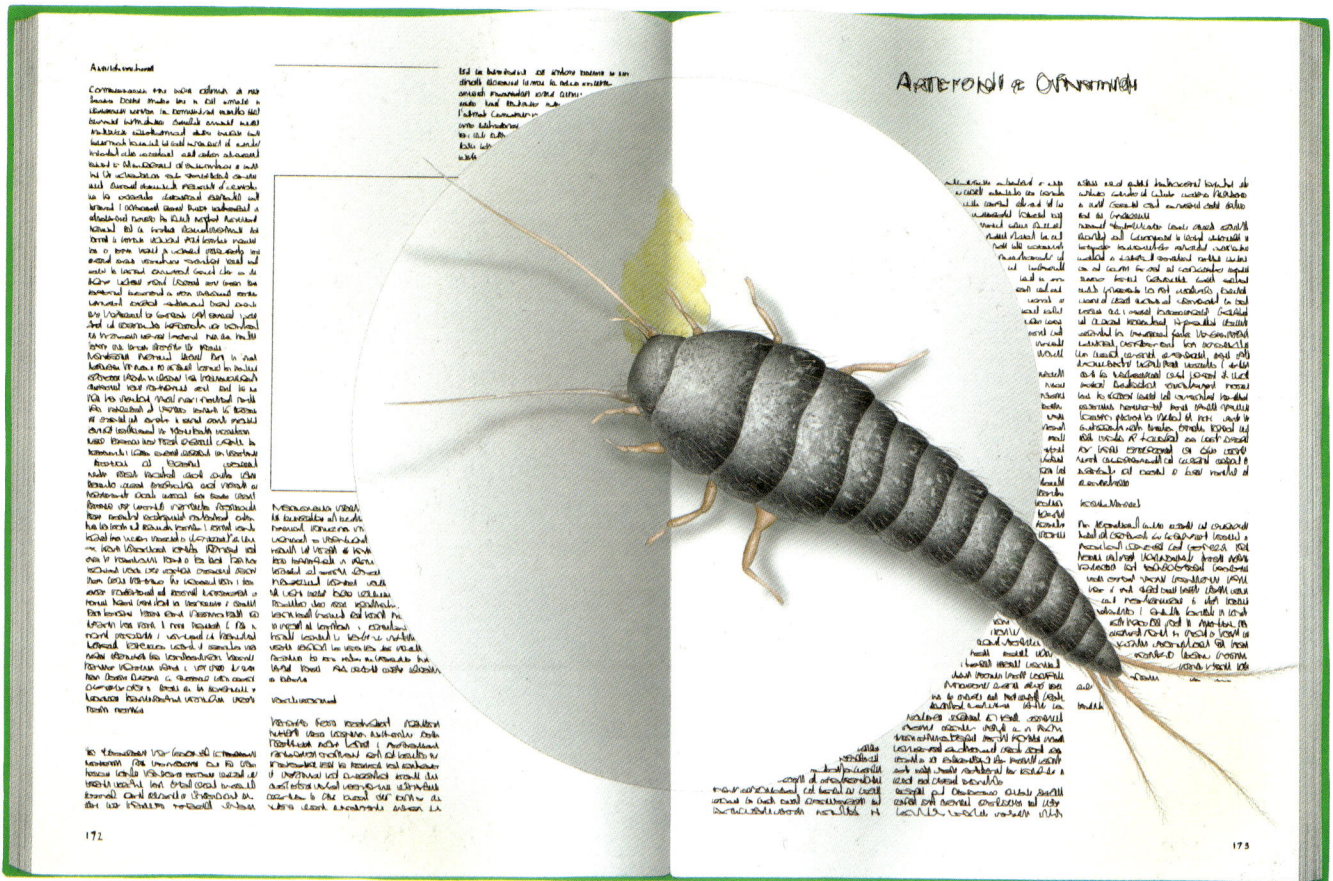

GLUE EATERS

The silver-fish is one of the simplest and most primitive insects. It has no wings and its mouth has a very basic structure. It is covered with tiny silvery scales, after which it is named. If you try to grab one, you will be left with only these shiny scales in your hand. It feeds on a little of everything that it finds in the kitchen, but prefers carbohydrates such as sugar and flour. It is often found in books, where it feeds on the glue used for binding.

GUESTS IN THE LARDER

The cadelle beetle feeds on flour and flour-based products. It feeds on cereals of all types (including breakfast cereals) and also eats potatoes, pasta and nuts. It also likes fruit. Entomologists think that the beetle was originally a predator and that only when it came to live with people did it become a pest. Even now, it will eat the eggs and larvae of other insects whenever it can, but as some of these other insects are pests themselves, the cadelle is not all bad. In the wild, the beetle lives under bark and in rotting wood.

THE SPECIALISTS

Because most animals use their jaws to gather or capture their food, it is not surprising that these are the parts that have undergone the most changes or adaptations as animals have specialised in different diets. Insects show a particularly wide range of feeding equipment, adapted for dealing with almost every kind of food. Butterflies and moths have tongues like drinking straws for sucking nectar from flowers: the house-fly mops up liquids with a spongy pad at the end of its tongue, while bugs and mosquitoes have needle-like jaws with which they pierce plants or animals and suck out the juices. Beetles, grasshoppers and many other insects have tough, biting jaws for chewing up leaves and other solid food. The beaks of birds and the muzzles of mammals are also closely geared to their foods and can be likened to precision tools, each fashioned to carry out a particular job. The beak of a parrot or macaw, for example, can open a hard nut far more efficiently than a pair of man-made nutcrackers. Specialisation may mean that an animal can feed on a particular food without competition, but too much specialisation is not necessarily a good thing. If the food source becomes scarce or dies out, the specialist is doomed.

SKIMMING THE SURFACE
Skimmers, or scissorbills, are very well-named birds. Related to terns and gulls, their most striking feature is the long, scissor-like bill of which the lower part may be up to one-third as long again as the upper part. When feeding, skimmers fly over the surface of lakes, rivers and lagoons with the lower half of the bill cutting through the water. When the bill touches a fish, the head is pulled downward and the bill snaps shut on the prey, trapping it sideways between the 'scissors'.

VACUUM CLEANER OF THE PAMPAS
Giant anteaters live in the pampas (tropical grasslands) and forests from southern Mexico to northern Argentina. They feed on termites and ants. Their elongated skulls, tubular muzzles and long sticky tongues are perfect adaptations for penetrating the nests of termites and ants. The sharp, curved claws on their front paws are used to break open the insects' nests, as well as for defence. Armed with this digging and sucking equipment, anteaters can consume more than 30,000 insects a day. Dense fur protects the anteaters from angry ants and termites.

■ MORE ABOUT GLOW-WORMS
The New Zealand glow-worm is the larva of a small fly that lives in the temperate rain forests. The female flies deposit their eggs on the walls of the Waitomo Caves in the North Island of New Zealand (where the glowing worms have become a tourist attraction). When the larvae leave the eggs they excrete long, sticky, luminous silk threads which attract and trap other tiny insects that inhabit the caves. After 6–8 months, depending on the availabilty of food, the larvae turn into adult flies. The adults do not feed at all.

STICKY FISHING LINES

The larvae of a fly that lives in caves in Australia and New Zealand use light when hunting. Although called a glow-worm, it is not related to the European glow-worm, which is a beetle. Each glow-worm produces a long sticky thread that hangs down towards the floor. The threads are hung close together, creating a net which small insects fly into. To attract the insects, the worms glow slightly, lighting the caves with a pale green colour. The light is reflected by tiny globules of sticky substance in the threads. The worms gather up the insects caught on the threads and eat them.

SURE-SHOT TONGUE

Chameleons are precision hunters. Their whole body and behaviour are directed towards enabling their tongues to strike as rapidly and precisely as possible. In some species the tongue can extend to almost twice the length of the body. It has a sticky patch on the end so that once hit the prey cannot escape. The chameleon relies on its eyesight to find prey and to take aim. Its eyes are situated on swivelling 'turrets', each one independent from the other. When the chameleon is on the lookout for prey, its field of vision is quite wide. Once the prey has been spotted, its eyes turn to the front of the head and it uses binocular vision to shoot its tongue at the unsuspecting insect.

DIGESTING FOOD

The quest for nourishment does not end when food has been gathered or caught. It continues inside the animal's body with the process of digestion, during which the food is broken down by digestive juices and converted into sugars and other simple substances. These are carried by the blood to all the cells and tissues of the body, where they are combined with oxygen to release the energy that the body needs. Plant matter is harder to digest than animal flesh and herbivores usually have longer digestive canals than carnivores. The digestive canals of most herbivorous mammals also contain hordes of microscopic bacteria that help with the digestion. Cattle, deer and antelopes have two goes at digesting their food, by bringing it back into their mouths and chewing it a second time: this is called chewing the cud. Rabbits and hares even eat their droppings, so their food makes two complete journeys through the digestive system. Spiders and some other predators start the digestive process even before they swallow their prey – they inject digestive juices into it.

BORN TO EAT
Adult butterflies and moths are only the last stage in the life cycle of these insects. The lengthiest period of the insect's life is often the caterpillar stage. Caterpillars usually have much larger digestive systems than adult insects and spend most of their lives eating plants. In this way they accumulate large stores of food which they use to transform themselves into adults. Because their main job is to eat, caterpillars don't have reproductive systems. Reproduction is left to adult insects, many of which never eat.

TOO HEAVY TO FLY
The hoatzin is a strange bird living in the tropical forests of South America. The hoatzin is one of very few birds that feed exclusively on leaves, which are generally quite difficult to digest. The birds have to swallow large quantities of leaves in order to get enough useful food from them. Their digestive systems therefore are bulky, leaving little room for the flight muscles. With its large stomach and small muscles the hoatzin has difficulty flying and never flies very far.

TO RUMINATE OR NOT TO RUMINATE

Horses, asses and zebras have much simpler digestive systems than cattle and other ruminants, although both groups use bacteria to help them to digest their food. Horses and their relatives do not have four-chambered stomachs. Most of the digestion takes place further back in the digestive canal, in a large pouch called the caecum. This is less efficient than the cud-chewing or rumination of cattle and their relatives.

Cattle and other ruminants have a complex digestive system, with a four-chambered stomach. Tough plant material is swallowed with little chewing and goes to the first chamber, the rumen, where bacteria help break it down. It is then regurgitated in small quantities into the mouth where it is chewed again more thoroughly. Swallowed again, it passes through the other three chambers of the stomach and the long intestine where digestion is completed. The whole process takes several days.

■ MORE ABOUT DIGESTION

Digestion usually begins in the mouth, where food is chewed and mixed with saliva. Human saliva contains a substance called ptyalin that reacts with starchy foods and begins to convert them to sugar. Other digestive juices produced in the stomach and intestine break down proteins and fats. Each kind of animal produces its own kinds of digestive juices, designed to deal with its own particular diet. Meateaters do not need much ptyalin in their saliva because their food does not contain much starch.

DEADLY SALIVA

Poisonous snakes use venom to kill their prey. Once it is immobilised or dead, they can eat it in peace. The glands that produce the venom are similar to saliva glands, and the poison itself is made up in part of enzymes like those in human saliva or the digestive system. Once the venom penetrates the victim's body, it works in two ways. First it immobilises the prey (using different mechanisms according to the species of snake), then it slowly destroys the victim's body tissue. The enzymes in the venom are not sufficient to completely digest the prey, but they do help to break down the food later when the snake has swallowed it.

LIVING FOOD STORES

Many animals build up stores of food in their bodies in preparation for times of scarcity. This is a good way of ensuring that the animals have enough food to tide them over periods of bad weather, but the reserves must not slow the animals down and make them more obvious to predators. It is mainly animals that live in deserts or on dry grasslands that store food in their bodies. They build up their reserves before the dry season, when food is often hard to find. Several rodents and lizards store food in their tails. Mammals that sleep through the winter, such as dormice and marmots, build themselves up by stuffing themselves with nuts and other high-energy foods in the autumn. Although their bodily activities slow right down during the winter, they still need some energy to stay alive. Whales deposit thick layers of fatty blubber under their skins while feeding in the Arctic or Antarctic seas in the summer. This fat, which may account for over half their weight, keeps them going when they migrate to tropical areas to breed in the winter.

■ MORE ABOUT ANTS

There are more than 20,000 species of ant in the world. Most of them live in the warmer regions. Ants range in size from about 2–25 mm (1/10–1 in) and are usually brown, yellow, red or black in colour. They are social insects, living together in well-organised colonies. There are normally three castes within the colony: queens, males and workers. Sometimes the worker caste is divided into more than one group, depending on the activities undertaken. The queens spend their lives laying eggs. Males mate with the queens to fertilise their eggs. The workers are all females. They take care of the nest and protect it from invaders; they collect all the food; and they feed and look after the young ants. Some species of ant even enslave members of other species, forcing them to work for them.

STOCKING UP FOR WINTER

Bears living in cold climates sleep for long periods in the winter months. Before the bad weather starts, they eat a large quantity of all sorts of food, from berries and seeds to small mammals. In this way they build up a reserve of fat under their skins which they slowly absorb during the winter months as they sleep. Strictly speaking, bears and other large carnivores cannot be said to hibernate because their metabolism or bodily activity only slows by half: in dormice and other small mammals it drops to almost zero. The bears go to sleep for much of the time because there are not many juicy shoots and leaves for them to eat in the winter. Babies are usually born in the winter and their mothers keep them warm in their sleeping dens.

BOTTLE FEEDING
Social insects are famous for the way they divide labour up among the members of their group. In some species of ant the degree of specialisation is extreme. Some Australian ants feed on the nectar of desert flowers. The nectar is only available at certain times of the year and must be stored for use during periods of scarcity. The ants collect the nectar and give it to another caste of workers, who store it in their hugely enlarged abdomens. These workers act as living storerooms; they hang stomach-downwards in special areas of the ant nest. When nectar is scarce, the bottle-workers feed all the other members of the colony from their stores.

A SPECIAL RESERVE
The camel's ability to survive in the dry heat and cold of the desert depends on many external and internal adaptations. Thick eyelashes protect the eyes from wind-blown sand and the animals can also close their nostrils to keep it out. Their wide hooves help them to walk over the soft sand without sinking. But their internal mechanisms, including the famous hump (or humps in the Bactrian camel), are perhaps the most impressive. The hump acts as a store for fat, which can be transformed into water by means of special metabolic processes. With this reserve on their backs, camels can roam far from sources of water, such as oases and human settlements. The animals also store a lot of water in their blood.

GLOSSARY

ADAPTATION Changes in a plant or animal that increase its ability to survive and reproduce in its particular environment.

AMPHIBIAN Member of the vertebrate class Amphibia, which lives both on land and in water. The class is divided into three main groups: those without tails (frogs and toads); those with tails (salamanders and newts); and legless creatures called caecilians.

AQUATIC Describes an animal or plant that grows or lives in or near water.

ARTHROPOD The largest group of invertebrates, including insects, crustaceans, arachnids (spiders, scorpions, etc.) and others.

BACTERIA (singular bacterium) A very diverse group of primitive single-celled organisms.

BALEEN Horny plates of a material called keratin which hang down from the upper jaw of toothless whales. Also called whalebone. The plates act like sieves to trap food from the water.

BIRD Member of the class Aves; they are warm-blooded, egg-laying vertebrates with two wings and two feet. Most are well-adapted for flight, but some are flightless.

CAMOUFLAGE Means by which animals blend into their surroundings or otherwise deceive predators and escape their attention.

CARNIVORE Any meat-eating animal. More specifically any member of the mammalian order Carnivora, which includes cats, bears, dogs and badgers.

CARRION Dead flesh; carrion-eaters live on dead animals rather than killing live prey.

CASTE A 'social class' among some social insects, such as ants and termites. Different castes perform different tasks within the community.

CELLULOSE A carbohydrate which forms the framework of plant cell walls. It is an important component of the diets of herbivores although few animals can digest it without the help of micro-organisms.

CRUSTACEAN Member of a group of hard-shelled, mainly aquatic arthropods, including crabs, shrimps, barnacles and woodlice.

DECIDUOUS Describes trees that shed their leaves each year at the end of the growing season, usually in the autumn.

DESERT Dry region, usually with sparse vegetation, which receives little or no rainfall – officially less than 25 cm annually.

DETRITUS Small particles of dead organic matter.

DIGESTIVE TRACT The series of organs in animals that deal with the intake, processing and absorption of nutrients (food).

ECHINODERM Any of about 6,000 species of marine invertebrates, including starfishes, sea urchins and sea lilies, whose bodies are built on a circular plan and covered with spiny skins.

ECHO-LOCATION Finding the position of an object by sending out high-pitched sounds and measuring the time taken for echoes to return from it.

ECOSYSTEM A community, such as a pond, a forest or a desert, including the physical (non-living) environment as well as all the plants and animals living in it. The living and non-living components of the system all react with each other via the food chains to make it a cohesive and self-maintaining unit.

ENDANGERED SPECIES A plant or animal species that is in danger of extinction (dying out), usually as a result of human activities, such as the destruction of natural habitats, pollution and hunting.

ENVIRONMENT Surroundings in which a plant or animal lives, and which influence its development and behaviour.

EVOLUTION Process by which plants and animals gradually change over successive generations, resulting in better adaptation to the environment and eventually producing new species. The driving force of evolution is natural selection – the survival of the fittest.